PERSPECTIVES ON EVOLUTION OF BUDDHISM

PERSPECTIVES ON EVOLUTION OF BUDDHISM

AN ANALYSIS OF THE CHINESE BUDDHIST TEXTS

PAPERS BASED ON CHINESE, PALI AND SANSKRIT SOURCES OF EARLY BUDDHISM

DR. (MRS.) SWATI GANGULY

Eastern Book Linkers

Delhi :: India

Published by :
EASTERN BOOK LINKERS
5825, New Chandrawal,
Jawahar Nagar, Delhi-7
Ph. : 3970287
E-mail : easternbook@mantraonline.com

Edition : 2002

ISBN : 81-7854-003-7

Laser Type Setting :
CREATIVE GRAPHICS
A-40/6, Gali No. 2,
Brahmpuri, Delhi-110053
Phone : 2195643

R.K. Offset Process, Delhi-32

PREFACE

In continuation with my studies on the fundamental *Abhidharma* texts preserved in Chinese, the present work proposes to examine various phases of the development of *Abhidharma* from original sources in Chinese, Sanskrit and Pāli in general, and from two of the fundamental *Abhidharma* texts preserved only in their Chinese versions entitled the *A-p'i-ta-mo-fa-yün-tsu-lun* (*Abhidharma-Dharmaskandha-Pādaśāstra*) and the *A-p'i-ta-mo-p'in-lei-tsu-lun* (*Abhidharma-Prakaraṇa-Pādaśāstra*) in particular. Both the text are lost in originals in Sanskrit and are preserved in their Chinese versions by Hsüan-tsang. The texts contain systematic treatment of the original teachings of the Buddha by the *Sarvāstivāda* school of Buddhism that highlight the initial phase of the development of Buddhist Philosophy and religion.

The relevant sections of the two Chinese texts as above have been translated into English for the first time to compare them with the *Abhidharma* texts in Pāli and Sanskrit in the present work. The *Abhidharma-Dharmaskandha-Pādaśāstra* is one of the earliest treasury of early Buddhism on the stages of the Buddhist Path attained through the moral, mental and intellectual disciplines. The *Abhidharma-Prakaraṇa-Pādaśāstra* unifies various doctrines of original Buddhism by classification and definitions of various theories and practices, thereby providing solutions to the problems posed by earlier *Abhidharma* texts. I sincerely hope that my humble attempt will help the students and researchers of Buddhist Studies to find a new direction to the studies on the evolution of early Buddhism.

I am thankful to the University Grants Commission for financial support extended to me since I carried out the study as an UGC Research Scientist "B" affiliated to the Department of Buddhist Studies, Delhi University, and the Asiatic Society, Calcutta. I am also grateful to the General Secretary, Staff and friends of the Asiatic Society for their co-operation without which this work would not have been possible. Thanks are due to Delhi University Library and Asiatic Society Library for granting me permission to use rare research materials. I am indebted to late Mr. Nihar Bhattacharya of Maxmuller Bhavan, Calcutta for his kind help to me in working with German sources.

The book in dedicated to the memory of my late mother in-law, Mrs. Maya Ganguly.

Swati Ganguly

ABBREVIATIONS

A, AN	:	*Aṅguttaranikāya*
ADPS	:	*Abhidharma - Dhātukāya - Pādśāstra*
ADSPS	:	*Abhidharma - Dharmaskandha - Pādaśāstra*
AK	:	*Abhidharmakośa*
AKB	:	*Abhidharmakośabhāṣyam*
APPS	:	*Abhidharma - Prakaraṇa - Pādaśāstra*
Aṭṭh	:	Aṭṭhakathā
AVS	:	*Arthaviniścayasūtram*
C	:	Chinese
D, DN	:	*Dīghanikāya*
DS	:	*Dharmasamgraha*
M	:	*Majjhimanikāya*
MSV	:	*Mūlasarvāstivāda Vinaya*
MV	:	Mah*āvyutpatti*
P	:	Pali
PTS	:	Pali Text Society
S	:	Sanskrit
Vibh	:	*Vibhaṅga*
Vis	:	*Viśuddhimagga*
T	:	*Taiso Shinshu Daizokyo*

INTRODUCTION

From the viewpoint of the development of early Buddhism during the growth of the various Buddhist sects in India, the seven fundamental *Abhidharma* texts of the *Sarvāstivādins* lost in their originals in India but preserved in Chinese, provide valuable sources on the techniques and methods adopted to arrange and interpret the Buddha's discourses for the solutions of the sectarian controversies on the same. Thus the texts grew up as an independent literature evolving the system of *Abhidharma.* A detailed examination of the texts indicate the different phases of the systematisation of the early Buddhist theory and practice. Strikingly, few major studies are done on the texts. Our study seeks to examine the Chinese, Sanskrit and Pali sources on the origin and development of *Abhidharma* with special reference to the seven texts in classical Chinese alongwith comprehensive analysis of some of the texts to reconstruct the salient features of the early Buddhist philosophy in India and China with special reference to the original *Abhidharma* and of the fundamental *Abhidharma.*

The paper on "Origin of *Abhidharma*" discusses the stages of the formation of original *Abhidharma* and the *Abhidharma Piṭaka* through gradual exposition of the Buddha's teachings collected in the Pāli *suttas*, the *Vinayas*, and the *āgamas* (Sanskrit counterparts of the *suttas* preserved in the Chinese) of the *Sarvāstivādins.* The meaning and usages of the word *Abhidharma* in these literature have been detailed in particular to show the first stage of the growth of *Abhidharma* by defining and classifying the doctrinal items. It initiated the analytical study of the categories like *skandhas*, *āyatana* and *dhātu* classified as mind and matter and the issue became a major topic of discussion in later *Abhidharma.* The opinion of the modern scholars of Buddhism regarding the systematisation of the seven *Abhidharma* texts of the *Theravādins* and the seven *Abhidharma* texts of the *Sarvāstivādins* on the basis of *mātikā* or *mātṛkā* (a list of topics) are critically discussed in the paper. It is likely that the thirty-seven *bodhipakṣīya dharmas* taught by the Buddha, considered as the most elaborated *mātṛkās* in the *Nikāyas* and the *Āgamas,* gave rise to the third *piṭaka* of the Buddhist literature. The *Ābhidhārmic* tendencies in the *Āgamas* and the *Nikāyas* are indicated by the use of technical terms, their definitions and etymologies and finally listing of them by methods of arrangements of the doctrimes. The paper also examines closely the aspects of the original *Abhidharma* comprising of the *sūtras* and *āgamas* marked with the *Ābhidhārmic* way of analysis. Finally, the arising of the different sects of Buddhism and the compilation of separate *Abhidharmapiṭaka* by the principal sects specially by the *Theravādins* and the *Sarvāstivādins* are discussed in a comprehensive manner.

The paper entitled "Development of the seven fundamental *Abhidharma* Texts in Chinese" deals with the seven fundamental *Abhidharma* texts of the *Sarvāstivādins* which are preserved in Chinese only excepting some fragments in original Sanskrit. After a detailed treatment on the date, authorship, contents, and historical background of the texts the characteristics of fundament-' *Abhidharma* are highlighted and the three stages of the growth of the fundmental *Abhidharma* are identified. So far as the development of the seven texts of the *Sarvāstivāda Abhidharma* are concerned, the *Saṅgītiparyāya,* the *Dharmaskandha* and *Prajñaptiśāstra* demonstrate the characteristics of early *Abhidharma,* the *Vijñānakāya* and the *Dhātukāya* that of the middle period, while the *Prakaraṇa-Pādaśāstra* and the *Jñānaprasthāna* that of the late period. The original *Abhidharma* was preoccupied with the annotation, elaboration, arrangement and systematisation of the Buddha's discourses. On the other hand, the fundamental *Abhidharma* introduced new techniques of classification, inclusion, exclusion, association, dissociation etc. New theories promoted by the *Sarvāstivāda* School were applied for the treatment of the contents of the original *Abhidharma*, so that the *Abhidharma* came to be studied in a more objective manner. Enquiry into the aspects of the physical and mental events became prominent in addition to their ethical and meditational values.

Among the early fundamental *Abhidharma* texts, the *Abhidharma-Dharmaskandha-Pādaśāstra* is considered as the most systematic treatment of *Abhidharma* developed by the *Sarvāstivāda* School. In the paper entitled "Early *Abhidharma* Philosophy and Practices : An Analysis of the *A-p'i-ta-mo-fa-yün-tsu-lun* (*Abhidharma-Dharmaskandha-Padaśāstra*)", the contents of the text are critically analysed to demonstrate the formation of the *Abhidharma* systems of thought and practices. The details of the contents show that the first fifteen chapter of the text elaborate the ethical doctrines leading to enlightenment and the rest six explain the theoretical doctrines related to insight. The first six chapters are concerned with instructions as they include the doctrines to be studied by the laymen and novices of the Buddha's teaching along with the attainment and fruits of religious life of an adept in the Buddhist path. The thirty seven *bodhipakṣīya dharmas* and other practices are highlighted in chapters 7-15. The doctrines of Buddhist philosophy like sense-organs (*indriyāni*), *āyatanāni*, *skandhas* etc., are specially discussed in chapters 16-21. The Chinese text of the *Dharmaskandha* is compared with parallel texts in Pāli and Sanskrit to identify some special features of the different *Ābhidhārmic* Texts belonging to different sects in different periods. For a clear understanding of the *Abhidharma* terminology used in the Chinese Text, a Sanskrit-Chinese-English Vocabulary is given at the end.

The *Abhidharma-Prakaraṇa-Pādaśāstra*, a text representative of the completion of the fundamental *Abhidharma* demonstrates the final categorisation of the Buddha's teachings. The last paper in the book, "An Exposition of the classification of Elements in the *Sarvāstivāda* text of the *A-p'i-ta-mo-p'in-lei-tsu-lun* (*Abhidharma-Prakaraṇa-Pādaśāstra*)" examines the contents of the Chinese version of the text comprising of classification of physical and mental elements pertaining to the Buddhist teachings. Classification of things was used in original *Abhidharma* but older method could not solve the problems arising with sectarian developments.

The text for the first time introduces a five-member classification of *dharmas*, i.e. *se* (*rūpa*), 2. *hsin* (*citta*), 3. *hsin suo-fa* (*citta*), 4. *hsin-pu-hsiang-ying-hsing* (*cittaviprayukta saṃskāra*), and 5. *wu-wei* (*asaṃskṛta*). *Rūpa* includes the four *ta-chung* (*mahābhūta*), the five *ken* (*indriya*) and the five sense objects (details in the paper), *Citta* comprises of the six *shih-shen* (*Vijñānakāya* or group of consciousness). Twenty seven *caittas*, sixteen *cittaviprayuktasaṃskāras* and three *asaṃskṛtas* are also classified. The items of the five *dharmas* are defined with further classification of each of them. The section on Classification of the ten knowledges (*chih, jñāna*) gives definitions of the ten forms of knowledge, i.e., *fa-chih* (*dharmajñāna*), lei-*chih* (*anvayajñāna*), *ta-hsin-chih* (*paracittajñāna*), *shih-su-chih* (*lokasamvṛtijñana*), *k'u-chih* (*duḥkhajñāna*), *tsi-chih* (*samudayajñāna*), *mieh-chih* (*nirodhajñāna*), *tsin-chih* (*kṣayajñāna*), and *wu-sheng-chih* (*anutpādajñāna*). "*Jñāna*" means here 'insight' which has a function to analyse and penetrate into the real nature of the world by knowing the true implication of the four Noble Truths, and by making known the fact of impermanency, miserableness, and unsubstantiality of all mental and material phenomena of existence. In its third section, the text presents the classification of twleve *āyatanas* (bases), i.e., 6 organs and 6 objects of sense, with consideration to *Ābhidhārmic* standards as to how many without *rūpa*, visible, invisible etc. (details in the paper). The relation of subordination of the old classification into five *skandha*, twleve *āyatanāni* and eighteen *dhātu* is also explained in detail. The fourth section explains the *skandha*, *āyatana* and *dhātu* and gives four new classifications in tens-

10 *ta-ti-fa* (*mahābhūmika dharma*), 10 *shan-ta-ti-fa* (*kuśalamahābhūmikadharma*), 10 *ta-fan-nao-ti-fa* (*kleśamahābhūmika dharma*), and *10 hsiao-fan-nao-ti-fa* (*upakleśamahābhūmika dharma*). The section also defines 6 *dhātu*, 5 *sparśa*, 5 *kleśa*, 5 *dṛṣṭi*, 5 *indriya*, 5 *dharma*, 6 *vijñānakāya*, 6 *sparśakāya*, 6 *vedanākāya*, 6 *saṃjñākāya* 6 *cetanākya*, and 6 *tṛṣṇākāya*.

The items treated in earlier *Abhidharma* treatise of the *Sarvāstivāda* are thus dealt in full and their deeper imports are considered. In its fifth section, the text deals with expositions of ninety eight *sui-mien* (*anuśaya*) or latent tendencies that tend to became conditions for the arising of ever new defilements. The twelve *anuśayas,* i.e. *kāmarāga, pratigha, rūparāga, ārūpyarāga, māna, avidyā, satkāyadṛṣṭi, antagrāhadṛṣṭi, mithyādṛṣṭi, dṛṣṭiparāmarśa, śīlavrata-parāmarśa,* and *vicikitsā.* make ninety eight. Among them 36 is confined to *kāmadhātu,* 31 to *rūpadhātu* and 31 to *ārūpyadhātu.* This constitutes a new classification. Section Six of the text gives an exposition of *jñeyadharma, anāsravadharma, anumeyadharma* etc. One thousand questions on various ethical and meditational practices of Buddhism are discussed in the seventh section. The eighth section is a résumé of the issues discussed in the entire text.

The *Prakaraṇapādaśāstra* bears the distinctive mark of *Abhidharma* as it unifies various doctrines of original Buddhism gradually shaped in the *suttas*/*sūtras* and the early fundamental *Abhidharma* texts like the *Dharmaskandhapādaśāstra* and the *Dhātukāya* etc. In it, the Buddhist terms are given exact definitions for clarification of concepts. The uniformity of explanations is thus achieved and the *Sarvāstivāda* gradually becomes a system of philosophy.

To summarise, our study examines the historical background, subject matter, methodology, philosophy and psychology of early Buddhism that went through various stages of development, i.e., the early period of the original *Abhidharma* and the three periods of the seven fundamental *Abhidharma* texts of the *Sarvātivādius.* Among the seven texts preserved in Chinese only, the early fundamental texts like the *Dharmaskandha* etc. seek to arrange, illustrate and define the theoratical and practical doctrines of the Buddha, relying heavily on earlier attempt by the *Nikāyas, Agamas* and the *Ābhidharmic sūtras.* The texts of the middle period like the *Dhātukāya* etc. introduce special techniques of analysis like inclusion, exclusion etc. of things to interpret the Buddha's teachings. Among the later *Ābhidharmic* texts, the *Prakaraṇapāda* is extremely analytic in character particularly in presenting a detailed scheme of classification of things besides giving exact definitions of the Buddhist terms to clarify the concepts of Buddhism. However, the texts on the whole show intense interest in exploring ethical, psychological and religious implication of human behaviour with the purpose of helping out a seeker to attain perfection in understanding. The nature and function of physical and mental processes are detailed for understanding the reality. Emphasis on psychological classifications points to the necessity of spiritual perfection. In the *Prakaraṇanpāda*, the questions and answers on the theory and practice of original Buddhism is thouroughly charged with religious consciousness of protecting and continuing with the Buddha's teaching for the time to come. The text thus marks the completion of *saddharma* as seen by the *Sarvāstivādins.*

CONTENTS

ORIGIN OF *ABHIDHARMA*

1. Meaning of the word *Abhidharma/ Abhidhamma*

The *abhidharma* signifies the title of the third *Piṭaka* (collection) of the Buddhist canon containing a number of texts compiled later than either of the two other *Piṭakas*, i.e., the *Sūtra Piṭaka*, and the *Vinaya Piṭaka.* The title *abhidharma* is also given to the content of those texts of the Third *Pitaka* and the specific method through which *dharma* as the doctrine of the Buddha is established in these texts, thus referring to a special type of commentaries on the *Sūras* known as the *śāstras* in the Sanskrit tradition of the Northern Buddhism.

The Third *Piṭaka* was finalised following the finalisation of the compilation of the First and the Second *Piṭaka.* So the word *abhidharma* found in the *Sūtra Piṭaka* and the *Vinaya Piṭaka* does not refer to the Third *Piṭaka.* For a clear understanding of the original concept of *abhidharma* used in the words of the Buddha and its development in the Third *Piṭaka*, the meaning of the term *abhidharma* is being discussed here.

A. Meaning of *Abhidharma* in Pali Buddhism

Etymologically the term *abhidhamma* is formed out of the prefix `*abhi*' and the noun `*dhamma*'. The prefix `*abhi*' means `to', `towards', `into' etc. and as a preposition it expresses `towards'. `with regard to', `one after the other' etc.[1] *Dhamma* (etymologically derived from the verb *dhr* `to hold', `to bear' etc.), in general refers to `doctrine', `teaching', `theory', discourse' etc. From philological point of view as accepted by W. and M. Geiger and others, *abhidharma* has been interpreted with the meaning of `concerning the *dhamma*, or refering to the *dhamma*' which is claimed to be the earliest meaning of *abhidharma*. In the Pali *Nikāyas*, *abhidhamma* appears in the locative case *(abhidhamme*, `with regard to *dhamma*') usually together with *abhivinaye* (concerning the *Vinaya*).[2] From this definition of *abhidhamma* (`concerning the *dhamma*'), the form of the same word is given as prepositional compound with the meaning of "as regard the *dhamma*."[3] This suggests the fact that the growth of *abhidhamma* is subsequent to *dhamma* and does not refer to the philosophical meaning of *abhidharma*.

2. The Word *abhidhamma* means "the special *dhamma*", i.e. the theory of the doctrine, the doctrine pure and simple (without any admixture of literary grace of personalities, or of arguments.......)[4]. In this case, the prefix *abhi* means `special' and functions as an adjective.

Abhidhamma thus has been translated as :

`The Advanced Teaching of Doctrine' (by C.A.F. Rhys-Davids in *Dialogues*, III, 246).

`Extra doctrine' and `further doctrine' (by F.L. Woodward in *Gradual Sayings*, I, 276 and V, p. 19, 139ff respectively).

`*More-dhamma*' (by E.M. Hare, *Ibid*., III. 85, IV. 267).

`Special-*dhamma*' and `further-*dhamma*' (E.J. Thomas in *History of Buddhist Thought*, pp. 159-276). ?

3. I.B. Horner points out that in the Pali canon the meaning of the word *abhidhamma* 'fluctuates' between 'concerning the *dhamma*' and the 'higher *dhamma*' and gives instancing examples by collecting the usages of *abhidhamma* and *abhivinaya* from the *Sūtra Pitaka* and the *Vinaya Pitaka*.[5] Critical details are available elsewhere,[6] in which it is established that Horner uses two expressions for *abidhamma*, i.e., 'Further-

Dhamma' and 'what pertains to *dhamma*'.

4. In the Pāli *Nikāyas*, we also have expressions like *abhidhammakathām kathaneti*[7] which is translated by Horner as 'talking on further *dhamma*'. Sometimes *abhidhammakathām* when used together with *vedallakathām*, talking on questioning' probably indicates 'an advanced discussion on *dhamma*.'[8]

5. In Pali commentarial literature *abhidhamma* means 'a special superior *dhamma*'. Thus in *Atth.* I, it is said by Buddha ghosa —"the prefix '*abhi*' is employed in the sense of excellence (*atireka*) and difference (*viśeṣa*), and *abhidhamma*, therefore means *dhamma* which excels (*dhammātireka*) and is differentiated (*dhammaviśeṣa*) from the other *dhamma* by its varied attributes."

The same author in his book *Samantapasādikā* (p. 20) gives five different meanings of *abhi*, *i.e.*, *vuddhi* (increase), *salakkhana* (characteristic), *pujita* (respect or worship), *paricchinna* (distinguishing) and *adhika* (excellence), and in examples of *abhi* mentions that '*abhi*' like "complete training in *abhidhamma* and *abhivinaya*, etc." is used in the sense of "distinguished" (*paricchina*). It is said that this is for the sake of getting rid of confusion between *dhamma* and *vinaya*; *abhi* indicating "with a beautiful (*abhikanta*) colour, etc." is in the meaning of excellent (*adhika*).

6. The word *abhidhamma* appears in the *Citta Sutta* (*A* III V, *sutta* 79), *Maha-Gosinga Sutta* (*M.* I. 214), *Gulissanit Sutta* (*M.* I. 472) etc. In the first two cases, *abhidhammakathāṃ* mean 'talks pertaining to the doctrine' while in the third case *abhidhamma* refers to 'pertaining to the *dhamma*.[9]

B. Meaning of *Abhidharma* in Early Buddhist Sanskrit Texts Preserved in Chinese

1. In the Chinese translation of *Madhyamāgama* (Sanskrit text belonging to *Sarvāstivāda* school) the word *gambhīra* (profound) is given as adjective before the word *abhidharma*.[10]

2. The word *abhidharma* is transliterated in Chinese as *a-p'i-ta-mo*, and is translated in various ways as the following :

ta fa	大法	great *dharma* or law
wu-pi-fa	無比法	peerless *dharma*
sheng-fa	勝法	excellent *dharma*
tuei-fa	對法	facing *dharma*
hsiang-fa	向法	proceeding *dharma*

Abhidharma is called 'great' because it is 'great knowledge of the four truths and destroys wrong views, ignorance, and delusions.' It is 'peerless *dharma* because of its teachings on 'eight forms of intelligence, ten forms of wisdom and the right view of purity which help to overcome the obstacles of the three realms of sentient beings.' *Abhidharma* is called 'excellent' because it reveals wisdom. It is again 'facing *dharma*' because of its cause-effect theory that cause proceeds to efect.[11]

3. The *Abhidharma- mahāvibhāṣā-śāstra,*[12] a principal compendium of the *Sarvastivada* school contains a long list of definitions of synonyms of *'abhidharma'*, including various explanations of *abhidharma* from the various sectarian traditions like the *Sarvāstivādins,*the *Mahīśāsakas,* the *Dharmottaras,* the Grammarians etc.

According to the *śabdavāda* or the Grammarians *a* means 'removal' and *bhi* designates discrimination. Thus *abhidharma* removes fetters (*gantha*), bad predisposition (*anuśaya*), secondary defilements (*upakleśa*), and prepossession (*paryutthāna*); one discriminates aggregates (*skandha*), sense organs, perception, their objects (*dhātu and āyatana),* causal law (*pratitya-samutpāda*), truth (*satya*), food (*āhāra*), the fruition of path (*śrāmaṇyaphala*), and *bodhyaṅga* (factors of enlightenment).

Buddharakṣita's theory holds that *abhi* means 'appearance'

and *abhidharma* draws all the good principles (*kuśaladharma*) causing various factors of enlightenment to appear.[13]

According to Buddhadeva *abhi*means 'predominance' and *abhidharma'* is called so because it is predominant.

In the opinion of Vāmalabdha, *abhi*means ' veneration' and *abhidharma* is called so because it is venerable.[14]

Vasumitra explains that, the *abhidharma* is called so because it analyses phenomena as expounded in the *sūtra* etc., along with twelve links of causal law, the Four Nobles Truths, the Eight Fold Path and enables one to realise *nirvāṇa.*

In the opinion of Mahābhadanta,the reason why it is called *abhidharma* is that, it 'collects', 'arranges', and ' discriminates' the *dharmas* such as *kleśas. ganthas, vimokṣa, nirvāṇa* etc.

In the opinion of Ghoṣa, the reason why *abhidharma* is called *abhidharma* is that it analyses the Four Noble Truths,the process of emancipation etc.

Pārśva opines that the reason why *abhidharma* is called *abhidharma* is that it treats of wisdom which express the ultimate and the excellent etc.

According to the *ābhidhārmikas* (one who preaches doctrines),the reason why the *abhidharma* is called *abhidharma* is that it treats of the real nature of subtle and profound *dharmas* and it is able to discriminate the characteristics of phenomena as well.

In the opinion of the *Mahiśāsakas*,the *abhidharma* is the highest knowledge that illuminates the phenomena.

According to the *Dharmagupta* school, *abhidharma* means 'increase', and' understanding which one is the best of all *dharmas*'.

According to the *Dārṣṭāntikas, nirvāṇa* is supreme to all *dharmas* and the *abhidharma* comes next to it.[15]

C. Meaning of *Abhidharma* inBuddhist Sanskrit Texts

1. Asaṅga in his *Mahāyānsūtrālankāra* (XI.3) explains *abhidharma* as *abhimukhato' thābhikṣṇyād abhibhavagatito' bhidharmaś ca.* This means *abhidharma* is:

   1. Being face to fact with highest goal and nature of reality (*abhimukha*).

   2. The teaching of necessary steps to be taken for attainment of the goal and presenting them from various viewpoints (*ābhikṣṇya*).

   3. Its standing above petty controversies about the nature of reality and its capacity to a definite answer (*abhibhava)*

   4. Penetration into the deeper import of the Buddha's teachings (*abhigati).*[16]

2. In his *Abhidharmakośa*[17], *Vasubandhu defines abhidharma* as *prajnā amalā sānucarā abhidharmaḥ* (*abhidharma* is pure wisdom with its "following" i.e., five pure *skandhas*). Commenting on this, Yaśomitra explains that *abhidharma* is pure transcendental knowledge of *citta, caitta, anāsravasaṃvara* (ethical observances for purity) and *cittaviprayukta* (mind-dissociated elements) and mentions that the text which deals with these topics is also called *abhidharma.*[18]

In short, *abhidharma,* in its primaray sense, is the pure (*amala*) wisdom (*prajnā*). But in its secondary sense is the knowledge that leads to pure wisdom, and this knowledge is the analysis of different aspects of mind enabling one to attain the perfect knowledge. In the latter sense, *abhidharma* means "*pertaining to dharma*" or "concerning the *dharma.*"

2. Traditional Account of the Origin of *Abhidharma*

In Pāli tradition, the Buddha is said to be the first

ābhidhārmika (*sammāsambuddho va pathamataram ābhidhammika, Aṭṭha.* 17). It is further mentioned that the seven Pāli *abhidhamma* texts were uttered by the Buddha himself (*lbid.*,3,5). On the origin of *abhidhamma,* another account describes how the Buddha revealed the *abhidhamma* for the benefit of his motherwhen he was residing in the heaven of Thirty-three Gods (*lbid.,1.76,1.360.*) According to the *Sarvāstivāda abhidharma,* the Buddha himself taught *abhidharma* in various occasions (*AK. 1.12 -evam abhidharma hi dharmalakṣaṇopadeśasvarūpo vineyavaśāt tatra bhagavatoktaḥ).*

The Aṭṭha (No. 32) observes that the *abhidhamma* taught by the Buddha was handed down to Sāriputta and successively to Bhaddaji, Sobhita, Piyajali, Piyadassi, Kosiyapautta, Sigggava, Sandeha, Moggaliputta, Visudatta, Dhammiya, Dasaka, Sonaka,Revata up to the Third Council and by theirpupils there on (*lbid*).From India, the *abhidhamma* tradition was brought to Ceylon by Mahinda, lthiya, Uttiya, Sambala and Bhaddasala, and was continued there by their pupils again (*lbid*).

However, as we have observed earlier that the term *abhidhamma* as used in the *Nikāyas* does not refer to a compilation of texts but to a special method of analysing the *dhamma.* So the claim that the Buddha himself was responsible for the literary form of the seven *abhidhamma* text does not seem to have a sound basis.

3. The *Abhidharma Piṭaka*

Various interpretations of the word *abhidharma* as mentioned earlier sugests that '*abhidharma*' meaning 'concerning the *dharma*' refers to 'discourse or discussion on *dhammas*' (*abhidhammakathā*) by 'definiting' or 'analysing (vi-*bhaj) dharmas,* by 'classifying '*dharmas* into different types *vibhaṅga)* or by arranging *dharmas* in numerical order

(*D.*111.207-71, *Saṅgitisutta, etc.)*, that was attempted by the Buddha and his disciples.[19] Those discussions were collected together in the *Abhidharma Piṭaka.*

Some scholars are of the opinion that those discussions concerning *dharmas,* their various classifications and itemizations were collected together as *mātikā or mātṛkā,* the earliest form of the *Abhidharma Piṭaka. The mātikā or mātṛkā* (literal meaning 'matrix') is a list of items of words which are made the objects of debate or discussion.

4. Mātṛkā and *abhidharma*

In the *Mahāparinibbāna sutta* (*D.*11,125; *T.1,17C,182C*) *mātikādhara* (versed in the doctrinal topics) is mentioned in addition to *dharmadhara* (versed in the doctrine) and *vinayadhara* (versed in the discipline). The word *mātikādhara* appears elsewhere (*A.*1.117; *M.*1.221 etc.) and in one place at least,the word *abhidhamma* is also used with it.

The term *mātṛka* used as a synonym for *'abhidharma'* is regarded as *Abhidharmapiṭaka* in the Chinese versions of the texts of the *Mūlasarvāstivāda Vinaya*[20], of the *Mahāsāṅghika Vinaya*[21], *and of the Sarvāstivāda Avadāna.*[22] In the first council, Kātyāyana himself decided to recite the *mātṛkā to* preserve the meanings of the *Sūtras Vinayas.* Then he recited thirty seven *bodhipakṣiya dharmas* (components of enlightenment, i.e., the four *smṛtyupasthānas,* the four *samyakprahānas,* the four *rddhipādas,* the five *indriyas,* the five *balas,* the seven *bodhyaṅgas, astāṅgika mārga).* After this he said,"know therefore, this is the *Sūtra,* this is the *Vinaya,* this is the *Abhidharma.*[23]" Thus *mātṛkā* is considered as thesimple form of the *Abhidharma Piṭaka.* As A.K. Warder observes that inthe earliest period,the third section of the *Tripiṭaka* probably consisted of only some set of *mātṛka* heading possibly preached by the Buddha as " systematic instruction" that was"later fully elaborated into *abhidharma* expositions.[24]"

The original *mātṛkās* are difficult to find in the *Nikāyas* and the *āgamas.* The list of seven topics arranging the thrity-seven bodhipakṣīya *dharmas* mentioned earlier seems to be the original *mātṛkā* which was delivered by the Buddha himself asthe summary of his doctrine at Vesali.[25] The 20 topics listed as the *mātikās* in the *MSV*(*T.*24,408b) may also have played important role in the growth of *abhidharma*[26]. In short, *mātṛka* is the systematisation of *dharmas* propounded in the *sūtras* and the *Vinaya* and thus is identified with *abhidharma.* In later period the *ābhidhārmikas* minutely analysed the items of *mātṛkā* and contributed exhastive treatment to each item.

However, one cannot absolutely claim that the *mātṛkās* mentioned above do not include all the topics covered in the *Abhidharma Piṭaka.* Besides, various dialogues in the *Nikāyas* and the *āgamas* collect various *dharmas* but do not use the word *mātṛkā.* Hence it may be said that though *mātṛkā* helped the growth of *abhidharma* but it did not 'directly develop the *Abhidharma* literature' (Pruden, *op.cit.*, p.xi).

The Japanese scholars (like Kimura) observe that the 'direct relationship with the later development of the commentarial literature on the *dhamma.* i.e.,the *abhidharma* commentaries lies with'discussion on the *dharmas*' (*abhidhamma-kathā*) practised in the early Buddhist *Saṅgha* (ibid.). Sometimes those discussions tended to ' summarise' and to 'itemise', whereas in some cases those discussions concentrated on 'analysis' and 'elaboration' of the *dharmas.*

5. *Ābhihārmic Āgamas*

The word āgama, in keeping up with its etymological meaning from the prefix *a*+the root *gam*" that which comes down" or " tradition", broadly refers to" a traditional doctrine or precept,a collection of such doctrines, sacred work." For the Buddhist, *āgama* is a general term for the original teaching of the Buddha transmitted through the traditional or canonical texts. Professor Nizumo mentions that the compilations of the original teaching of the Buddha,i.e., the five *Nikāyas* and the four *āgamas* are collectively known as the *āgamasūtras.*[27] It is belived that with the rising of the sects those *āgamās* or transmitted doctrines were called as the *nikāyas* (compilations) otherwise known as the Sutta *Piṭaka* compiled by the *Theravādins,* The *Sarvastivādins* however , mainatained the term *āgamas* for the compilation of their *Sūtra Piṭaka.*

Poussin observes that precanonical Buddhism promoted the popular teaching of the Buddha. The subtle teachings of the Buddha were not preached but were preserved in the texts which were studied by the monks in the monasteries and were transmitted from generation to generation. These texts are called '*āgamas*' or *āgamasūtras* referring to both the collections of the *Nikāyas* and the *āgamas* that contain the subtle or the philosophical teaching of the Buddha. Stcherbatsky, however, maintains that the Buddha's teaching that permitted the divergence of opinions among the Buddhist monks who gradually isolated themselves in various sects. Thus there is no basic difference between early Buddhism and *Abhidharma* Buddhism[28] so far as their 'elitist' and 'formal' natures are concerned.

6. *Ābhidhārmic* Tendencies in the *āgamas* and the *Nikāyas*

The scholars have already noticed those tendencies leading to the systematisation of the *āgamas* into the *nikāyas* or compilations.[29] The doctrines transmitted through those *āgamas* texts were later collected formally with the use of technical terms. Later the terms were analysed in det ails with definitions (*Vibhaṅga*) and etymologies (*nirukta*). Later o n these terms were systematised into *mātrkās* by (1) using numerical categories,or (2) showing similarities of the subject-matter of different texts, or (3) elaborating the *suttas* or *agamas.*

In the first case one can see listing of items in a list from one to ten in the *Saṃgītisuttā nta* in D. and in the *Dasuttarasuttānta* in D 34. The *A.* classifies its *suttas* on the basis of numerical categories (group of four items). The example of the second case is *Salāyatanavagga* in the *M*, in which all the texts dealing with *āyatanas* were grouped together. These texts are known as *saṃyukta/saṃyuta* (conjoined) texts. The characteristics of elaboration or extended commentary (*vibhaṅga*) is observed in the *sutta* of *S.*XII.2. which is an extension of XI.2. The *āgamas* having the characteristics of *vibhaṅga* are closely identified with their Pali counterparts.

The *āgmasūtras* with the tendency of systematising the teaching of the Buddha including commentary and systematised *sūtras* are the earliest form of *abhidharma* or the original *abhidharma*. Those *sūtras* are also called the *ābhidhammika* (*abhidhārmika*) *sutra*[30] that eventually led to the growth of *abhidharma* as a separate literary genre which is known as the fundamental *abhidharma* that was collected in the various *Abhidharma Piṭakas* of the canon belonging to various schools of Buddhism.

7. Original *Abhidharma*

In general the subject matter of original *abhidharma* includes the thirty seven *bodhipakṣīya dharmas,* Four Truths and *pratītyasmutpāda* as the theory of causation. Sariputra, the early researcher on *abhidharma* deals with various subjects of dispute like difference between wisdom and ignorance,i.e., understanding(*paññā),* consciousness (*viññāna*), sensation (*vedanā*), perception (*saññā*), right view (*sammā diṭṭhī*), the three realms of existence (*dhātu),* the four stages of meditation (*jhāna*), attainment of extinction (*nirodha)* and three forms of emancipation. In the *Cūlavedalla* sutta[31] of the *M.* the following topics are discussed - the five *khandhas,* individuality (*puggala),* relation of the eight fold path with the three studies (*sīla, samādhi, paññā),* the difference between the conditioned (*saṅkhāta*), and the unconditioned (*asaṅkhāta*), the attainment of *nibbāna* etc. These may well be called the topic of *abhidharma.*

The systematic exposition of the above topics is found in the *M.* The *Bahudhātuka Sutta*[32] expounds the functions of the eighteen *dhātus* (elements), twelve senses and objects, twelve link of causation (*paticcasamuppāda*). The Chinese translation of the *Sūtra* (F.N. 32) treats four applications of mindfulness and the seven factors of enlightenment in addition. The *Chachakka Sutta* (*M.*111.280-87, Chinese version *Tl*, 790b-792b) deals with the six sense organs, the six sense objects, the six kinds of touch (*phassa*), the six kinds of craving (*tanhā*), *paticcasamuppāda* or the conditions for the suffering and the course of their extinctions.

The distinct characteristics ofthe original *abhidharma* are threefold -(a) annotation and elaboration by giving definitions and explaininag terminology, (b) arranging and classifying numerical doctrines according to numerals, and (c) systematisation of the doctrines.

For (a), the examples of a series of *Vibhaṅga Sūtras* conatining eight *sūtras*[33] may be cited. The eight *sūtras* are:

Cūlakammavibhaṅga
(Ying wu Ching) 鸚鵡經

Mahākammavibhaṅga
(Fen pieh ta yeḥ Ching) 分別大業經

Uddesavibhaṅga
(Fen pieh kuan fa Ching) 釋法

Salāyatanavibhaṅga
(Fen pieh liu ch'u Ching) 分別六處經

Araṇnavibhaṅga
(Chü lou Shou wu Cheng Ching) 拘樓瘦無諍

Dhātūvibhaṅga
(Fen pieh liu chieh Ching) 分別六界經

Saccavibhaṅga
(Fen pieh sheng ti Ching) 分別聖諦經

Dakkhiṇāvibhaṅga
(Ch'u t'an mi Ching) 瞿曇彌經

Each of them presents detailed definitions and enumeration of doctrines as *karma*, inner and outer sense organs, the six worlds and the four truths. Some of them were taught by the Buddha himself in brief and then were detailed by his disciple. Forexample, the *Uddesa-vibhaṅga sutra*[34] demonstrates how Mahā-Kaccāna defined in detail the *dharmas* following the Buddha's brief statement on them.

The (b), that is arranging *dharmas* in numerical order,is illustrated by the *Saṅgītisutta*,the *Dasuttarsutta* and their Chinese versions. The *Ekottarasutta* which is available only in Chinese translation[35], also belongs to the above group. These *sūtras* are collections of definitions and various doctrinal principles. In the *Sangitisutta*[36], the *mātikās* are classified in the order of ones, twos, threes etc, up to tens. The *Dasuttarasutta*[37] lists items in a list from one to ten. The *Ekottarasūtra* enumerates items classified according to the numbers of the items in sections of one.... up to elevens. The *A*,as mentioned earlier, is also mainly a collection of items arranged in numerical order.

The (c), that is systematisation of the doctrines of the Buddha may be specially noticed in the *Chachakkasutta*[38] which has been dealt elsewhere.[39]

8. The Buddhist Sects and *Abhidharma piṭaka*

Ābhidhārmic tendencies found in the dialogues of the Buddha were extended and developed in to a comprehensive and consistent body of doctrine by the Buddhist theorists of different sects while preparing their own systematic works on *abhidharma.* The *abhidharma* texts were produced after the separation of sects which took place covering a considerable period of time. The Chinese text *I* 異 *pu* 部 *tsung* 宗 *lun lun*[40] 論(*T.*2031) records the earliest division of Buddhist Saṅgha into two schools, i,e., *Sthaviravāda* (*shang pu*) and *Mahāsāṅghika* (ta *chung pu*) during the period of Asoka. *Sthaviravāda* again was divided into two schools, i,ẹ., (*shuo i chieh yu pu*), and original (*mūla*) *Sthaviravāda* (*ken pen shang tso pu*). Out of those divisions other schools also emerged and the older schools wanted to make their positions stronger as a result of which the school ofthe *Sthaviravāda* and the *Sarvāstivāda* developed their own *abhidharma* literature. Both the schools had little disagreements over their *Sūtras* and *Vinayas* as they were all derived from a common source. But the wide divergence of the contents and methods of their *abhidharma* literature shows that the later was compiled independently whenthe two schools were separated geograpically.

The *Sthaviravādsa* claims the following seven texts as constituting its *Abhidharma piṭaka.*

1. *Dhamma-saṅgani* "Enumeration of the *Dhammas*"
2. *Vibhaṅga* "The Book of Treatise"
3. *Dhātu-kathā* "Discussion of the Elements"
4. *Pugala-paññatti* "Description of Individuals"
5. *Kathā-vatthu* "The Book of Controversy"
6. *Yamaka* "Clarification of expressions" or " Book of Pairs"
7. *Paṭṭhāna* " The Book of Origination"

Of the schools that contributed much for the development of *abhidharma,* is the school of *Sarvāstivāda (i chieh yu pu),* the 'All Exist'(*sarvam asti*) school which branched off from the *Sthaviravāda* following a schism towards the end of the reign of emperor Aśoka (probably around 237 B.C.). The name of the school is derived from its doctrine that all the principles exist (*i chieh yu)* and this existence includes also the existence of past and future occurrence of the principles. The *Sarvāstivādins* also had seven fundamental *abhidharma* texts:

1. *Abhidharma* - *Saṅgiti paryāya-pāda-śāstra*
2. *Abhidharma* - *Dharma-skandha-pāda-śāstra*
3. *Abhidharma* - *Vijñānakāya -pāda-śāstra*
4. *Abhidharma* - *Dhātukāya-pāda-śāstra*
5. *Abhidharma* - *Prakaraṇa-pāda-śāstra*
6. *Abhidharma* - *Prajñapti-pāda-śāstra*
7. *Abhidharma* - *Jñānaprasthāna-śāstra*

Among these textsthe *Jñānaprasthāna* is themost detailed text onthe topics treated in six other texts. The scholars believe that the *Jñānaprasthāna* was the most important text like the body whereas the six other works were shorter dealing with topics. These are known as the "legs" in relation to the *Jñānaprasthāna.*

About 286 B.C. , a' new recension of the *Abhidharma* in nine sections' prepared by monk Vātsīputra is claimed to have a transmission of teaching from Sāriputra and Rāhula.[41] The followers of Vātsīputra, the *Vātsīputrīyas* formed a new Buddhist sect, apparently on the basis of the doctrines formulated in the above text, specially on the doctrine of *pudgala*(person) in which the latter was accepted as a reality.

It is further reported that the study of the *Abhidharma* in nine sections was added with new texts produced by four new schools,i.e., The *Dharmottarīya, Bhadrayānīya, Sāmmitiya, and Sannñāgarika.* Among them the *Abhidharma* text, the *Aśrayaprajñapti śāstra* or *Sāmmitiya śāstra* is preserved in a

Chinese translation (*T.*1649).[42]

Among the subsects of the *Mahāsaṅghikas,* the *Gokulika* (variants Kaukutika, Kaurukullaka etc.) held the identical views with the *Vātsiputriyas.* This has been confirmed by Bhāvya, Vinītadeva, and Vasumitra.[43] Paramārtha inhis Chinese translation of the *Samayavedoparacancakra* gives the view of the Gokulika on *abhidharma* that holds that it is the *Abhidharma Piṭaka* that contains the real teachings of the Buddha, and thus is themost reliable among the three *piṭakas.*

Towards the end of the third century,B.C., the *Gokulika*was divided into two branches,i,e., the *Bahuśrutīya* and the *Prajñaptivāda,* most likely through the '*abhidharma* type of discussion'. The *Bahuśrutīya* was affiliated to the *Satyassiddhi* school of Harivarman.[44] The *Tattvasiddhi* by Harivarman representing the *Bahuśrutīya* is a late text. However the method of *mātṛkā* in the work presupposes a similar *abhidharma* text of the *Bahuśrutīyas.* The *Prajñaptivāda* possessed a 'special *abhidharma śastra*' that explained *sūtra* by distinguishing various kinds of statements in it.'[45]

Among the other Buddhist schools, the *Dharmaguptaka* school (*Fa tsang pu*) and the *Kāśyapīya* school are said to have their own *Abhidharma piṭaka* in four sections.[46] The Dharmaguptaka's four sections on *abhidharma* are : (1) Difficult (texts), (2) Not difficult (texts), (3) *Saṃgraha* ('inclusion'), and (4) *Saṃyukta* ('conjoined'). The four sections of the *Kāśyapiyas* are: (1) *Sapraśnaka vibhaṅga* (with questions), (2) *Apraśnaka vibhaṅga* (with out questions), (3) *Saṁgraha*, and (4) Camparative tables.

The *Sāriputrābhidharma śāstra* preserved in Chinese (*T.1548)* that belongs to the *Dharmaguptakas* also has four sections,i,e., *Sapraśnaka, Apraśnaka, Samykta-saṁgraha (dharmas*'occurring together and inclusion in classes as two basic kinds of relations' between *dharmas*) and *Nidāna* ('source') or *Prasthāna* (study of conditions).

The *Saṅgitiparyāya śāstra* is generally taken as the earliest *abhidharma.* It is a list of *dharmas* mentioned in the *sutras* grouped in one,two,three etc, and the *dharmas* are explained by quoting the *sutras.* The *Sapraśnaka* emerged from the theoretical list of the *skandha, āyatana* and *dhātu, āryasatya* etc, explained by *abhidharma*-analysis. *Prasthāna* deals with four conditions,i,e.,*hetu, ālambana, anantara* and *adhipati* which were accepted as the four original conditions by the *Sarvāstivāda, Sthaviravāda,* and the *Dharmaguptaka.* The development of the four sections of original *abhidharma* inthe *abhidharma* has been discussed elsewhere.[47]

The elaboration of *abhidharma* by different sects of Buddhism grew up around the various texts of their *Abhidharma Piṭaka* produced in various phases of the growth of *abhidharma.* For the *Sarvāstivādins,* the *Saṅgitiparyāya,* the *Dharmaskandha,* parts of the *Dhātukāya* and the *Vijñānakāya* probably form their original *abhidharma.* After the emergence of the *Sarvāstivāda* school, the *Sarvāstivādin* monks composed further *abhidharama* texts of their *Tripiṭaka.* The ealier texts demonstrate close resemblance with the *sūtras* or the doctrines of the Buddha while the later texts bear the sectarian characteristics ofthe *Sarvāstivādins* who tried to establish their own positions.[48]

RÉSUMÉ

In sum, *abhidharma* being a gradual annotation and explanation on theBuddha's teaching (*sūtra)* and precept (*vinaya)* grew up in the Pāli *Nikāyas* and the *Sarvāstivāda āgamas.* Discussion on *Abhidharma* and *abhivinaya* found in the various *sūtras* were used to develop the doctrine and to define the *dharmas.* Besides, the usage of the words like *Abhidhammakathā* etc., in certain *sūtras* in the *Nikāyas* and the *āgamas,* contain doctrinal items classified according to the numerical order. This indicates the early phase of *abhidharma* in which analyical study of *skandhā, āyatana, dhātu* etc., the classification of mind and matter by those categories, causation etc,are established.

The summary of doctrine given by the Buddha himself at Vesali gave rise to the idea of a *mātṛka* (a list of topics) and gradually the various elaborations of *mātṛkā* developed to *abhidharma.* The most detailed *mātṛkās* in the *Nikāyas* and the *āgamas* are the thirty seven practical *dharmas* (*bodhipakśiya dharmas*) connected with practice and emancipation., Thus the organisation of the Buddha's teachings by his disciples through the synthesis of analysis and practice marks the beginning of the study of *abhidharma.* This was further advanced during the emergence of the various schools of Buddhism and the collection of the *Tripiṭaka,* specially that of the *Abhidharma Piṭaka* by the *Sthaviravāda and the Sarvāstivāda* school.

Notes

1 Geiger, M and W., *Pāli Dhamma,* Munich, 1921,pp,118-19.

2 *D.*111.267:*M.I.472etc.*

3 *Critical Pali Dictionary*, 1935, P. 350.

4 *Pali English Dictionary* (*PTS*, 1st edition 1921-25 ,p.65). Also see G.P. Malalasekera, *Dictionary of Pali Proper Names,* London,1937-38.

5 See her article "*Abhidhamma abhivinaya* in the First Two *Piṭakas* of the Pali Canon" , in *Indian Historical Quarterly,*Vol.XVll, No,3,1941 pp.219-310

6 See Leo M. Pruden's introduction to his English tr, of the French version of the *Abhidharmakośabhāsyam* by Pousin, California, 1988, pp.XXXl-XXX111.

7 *M.I., p.214.*

8 *A.111.107.* For details see Watanabe, *Philosophy and*

its Development inthe Nikāyas and Abhidhamma, Delhi, 1983, p. 31-32. Also *Encyclopaedia of Buddhism,* (ed).G. Malalasekera. on '*Abhidharma*', *p.39.*

9. Encycolpaedia, *Ibid.*

10 *T.1,450a, 634c,728c etc.*

11 Encyclopaedia,*op.cit., pp.39-40.*

12 Tr. into Chinese (*T.*Vol, 27, 1545) by Hsüan-tsang between 656 A.D.and 659 A.D.).

13 *Ibid., T.*, 4b

14 *Ibid .*, 4C.

15 *ibid., Vol.28, 3c, 4a.*

16 Quoted from H.V. Guenther, *Philosophy and Psychology in the Abhidharma,* Delhi, p.2.

17 *AK., 1.2.*

18 *AKV.*, p.11

19 See Watanabe, *op.cit.*, p.36.

20 *Ken pen shuo ichieh yu pu p 'i nai yeh (T.*24,p.408b)

21 *Mo ho seng chih lu* (T.22. p.334).

22 *Aśokāvadāna in Chinese (T.50.p. 113*C).

23 Translation by Pruden, *op.cit., p.* XXXIX.

24 Warder,*0p.cit.,* p.10

25 *Ibid.,* p.11.

26 Watanabe,*op.cit.*,p.45

27 Kogen Nizumo, *Buddhist Sūtras,* Tokyo, 1982, p.16. For details, see Swati Ganguly, 'The Meaning and

Scope of *āgama* in Buddhist Literature' (unpublished paper), Delhi.

28 See his *Conception of Budhiṣt Nirvāṇa,* Delhi, 1989, pp.2-3.

29 Watanabe, *op.cit.*

30 *Encyclopedia, op.cit.,* p.43

31 *M.l,* pp.292-98 and its Chinese version in *T.*1,790b-792b.

32 *M.*1.pp.299-305, Chinese version in *T.*1,788a-790b.

33 For details of Pali version see *M.*111.pp.202-257. For a short analysis of the eight *sutras,* see B.C. Law, *A History of Pāli Literature,* Vol.1, Delhi, 1983, p.153-155.

34 *M.*111, 223-229. For Chinese version see *T.l.,* 694b-696b.

35 *Tseng yi a han ching, Nanjio,* No.534.

36 *D.*111, pp.207-271.

37 *lbid* ., pp.272-293.

38 *M.*111,280-287. Chinese version *T.l.,* 562a-566a.

39 Encyclopaedia, *op.cit.,*p.66. Also Watanabe, *op.cit.,* pp.54-55.

40 Skt. title *Samayabhedoparacanacakra.* It is translated from Chinese into English by J. Masuda in the *Asia Major,* 1925, Vol.11.pp. 1-78. The original text in Sanskrit composed by Vasumitra is lost.

41 Lamotte, *HBl,* pp.209, 487.

42 Translated from Chinese by K. Venkataraman in *Visvabharati Annals.*

[43] Details in N. Dutt, *Buddhist Sects,* p.49.

[44] See his *Tattvasiddhi śāstra* in Chinese Version (*T*1646).

[45] Warder, *op.cit.,* p.278.

[46] Cf.N.Dutt, *Buddhist Sects,* pp.171, 173.

[47] See Warder, *op.cit.,* p. 221-223; Watanabe, *op.cit.,* pp.63-64.

[48] *Ibid .,* pp.342-44.

DEVELOPMENT OF THE SEVEN FUNDAMENTAL *ABHIDHARMA* TEXTS OF THE SARVĀSIVĀDINS

1. Seven *Sarvāstivāda Abhidharma* Texts Preserved in Chinese

The seven texts of the *Sarvāstivādin Abhidharma Piṭaka* were, in all probability, composed in Sanskrit language as the *Sarvāstivādins* adopted Sanskrit for their literary activities. Unfortunately all the originals of the texts excepting a few fragments are lost and are preserved only in their Chinese versions as the following:-

1. *A-p'i-t'an-pa-chien-tu-lun and A-p'i-ta-mo-fa-chi-lun'.*

2. *A-p'i-ta-mo-chi-i-men-tsu-lun.*

3. *A- p'i-ta-mo-fa-yün-tsu-lun.*

4. *A-p'i-ta-mo-shih-shen-tsu-lun*

5. *A-p'-ta-mo-chieh-shen-tsu-lun.*

6. *A-p'i-ta-mo-p'in-lei-tsu-lun* and *Chung-shih-fen-a-p'i-tan-lun.*

7. *Shi-she lun.*

Those are the Chinese titles for the *Abhidarma Jñanaprasthāna-sāstra*, the *Abhidharma Saṅgītparyāyapāda-śāstra*, the *Abhidharma Dharmas kandhapāda-śāstra*, the

Abhidharma Vijñānakāyapāda-śāstra, the *Abhidharma-Dhātukāya-pādaśāstra*, the *Abhidharma Prakaraṇapāda-śāstra*, and the *Prajñaptipādā-śāstra* respectively.

The Chinese versions of the *Jnānaprasthāna*-by Saṃghadeva and Chu-Fo-mien in 383 A.D. exists in T. 1543 where as the same by Hsuan-tsang in 657-660 A.D. exists in *T.* 26 No.544. The two translations bear different names of the original text. The first is *Aṣtagrantha* (*pa chien tu*) where as the other is '*Abhidharma-śāstra*'. Paramārtha (499-569 A.D.), the famous Indian monk and translator of Buddhist texts in Chinese also mentions two names of the works in his' Life of Vasubandhu'. Modern scholars, however, maintain that the two works represent two different traditions of *Sarvāstivāda Abhidharma*, i.e., the Kashmiri *Sarvāstivāda* and the Gandhara *Sarvāstivāda.* The *Aṣta-grantha* is believed to represent the former tradition while the latter is represented by the *Abhidharma-śāstra.* The commentaryon the *Jnānaprasthāna* is also available in two Chinese translations. The commentary from Kashmir is known as the *Mahā-Vibhāṣā* (*Ta p'i- she lun T.*1545) whereas the commentary from Gandhara is termed as the *Vibhāṣā* (p'i po she *T.*1546).

The *Vibhāṣā* and the AKB mention that the teachings of the Buddha scattered through the scriptures were collected by Kātyāyanī putra in the *Jñānaprasthāna.*[1]

According to Hsüan -tsang, Kātyāyanīputra or Kātyāyana (ko ta yen na) composed the *Jñānaprasthān-śāstra* in the monastery of Tāmasavana in North India about three hundred years after the *parinirvāṇa* of the Buddha, However, Poussin quotes from the *Vibhāṣā* (T.26,p.21c 29), a commentary on the *Jñānaprasthāna*, which mentions that Kātyāyanīputra lived in eastern part of India during his composition of the *Jñānaprasthāna* as the latter cites an examples of the five rivers which are 'known in the east.'[2]

Takakusu assumes that the original text of the

Jñānapasthāna brought by Saṃghadeva and Dhammapiya seems to have 'been in a dialect akin to Pāli' where as the text translated by Hsüan tsang was probably in Sanskrit[3]; . Poussin observes that quotations by Yaśomitra on the Chapters of the *Jñānaprasthāna* named as *skandhaka* refer to the text in Sanskrit.[4] A Sanskrit fragment found by Pelliot was identified as that of the *Abhidharma-Jñānaprasthāna-śāstra* by Demieville (*Journal Asiatique*, CCXLIX, 1961, pp.461-75). The *AKV.* (11.10,16,26,36.....Vll,2,12 etc) quotes Sanskrit fragments of the *Jñānaprasthāna.*[5]

A preface of the earlier translation of the text written by Tao-an mentions that the original Indian text (*fan Pan*) consisted of 15,072 *ślokas* (*shou lu*) or 482,304 syllables (*yan*).[6]

At the end of each of eight fassiculi of Hsüan-tsang's translation of the text it is stated that thetext belonged exclusively to the *Sarvāstivāda* school. The monastery of Tāmasavana visited by Hsüan -tsang was also a seat of the *Sarvāstivādins.*

The *Jñānaprasthāna* consists of the basic *Sarvāstivādin* doctrines which were developed in later *Abhidharma* literature. Because of this, the text is known as the *mūla-śāstra* (*pen-lun*) and the basic *Abhidharma* treatise (*ken-pen-a-p'i-ta-mo*).

The *Jñānaprasthāna* is divided into eight sections. The first section contains the exposition of Transcendental knowledge (*shih ti yi fa*), knowledge (*chih*), Individuality(*pu tu chieh lo,i.e., pudgala*), Respect, Shamelessness (*Wu kuei*), characteristics (*hsing*), objectlessness (*Wu yi*), and Thought (*szu*). The second section details the Connections (*saṃyojanas, chieh*) which obstructs the spiritual progress of an adept, and are the causes of connections or defilements. The third section is devoted to the attainment of knowledge (*chih*), i.e., the branches of Buddhist learning, right and wrong views, knowledge of other mind, cultivation of knowledge etc. The fourth section on *karma* deals with evil actions and their consequences. It also discusses the visible and the invisible (*avijñapti*). The fifth details the four great elements and their products, both external and internal. The sixth section explains the controlling Faculties (*indriya*) and the three spheres of existence. The seventh section deals with various mental states of an adept while passing to the higher stage of non -returner from the stage of once-returner in meditation. The eight section gives details of the four Applications of mindfulness,the various wrong views etc.

The Chinese version of the *Saṅgitiparyāya-pāda-śāstra,*[7] i.e., the *A-p'i-ta-mo-chi-i-men-tsu-lun* by Hsüan tsang was done in 660-663 A.D.and exists in *T.* 26, no.1536. The original text is attributed to Mahakauṣṭhila by Yaśomitra and Bu-ston, and to Sāriputra by Chinese writers. Takakusu remarks that the text was compiled by Mahākauṣṭhila after the Council of Vesali which was held to reprimand the rules concerning the ten points of discipline.[8] The *Dharma,* i.e.,the doctrines and the discipline, were arranged in numerical order of *ekottara,* (increasing the numbers one to ten gradually).

Poussin[9] and other scholars have observed that the *Saṅgītiparyāya* is a recension of the *Saṅgītisuttnāta* of the *Dīghanikāya.* In contents it agrees with the *Dasuttarasuttānta* of the *Dīghanikāya,* and in form it closely resembles with the *Sthaviravāda Abhidhamma* text of the *Pugalapaññatti.*

At the end of the *chuans* 2-18 and 129-20 of the Chinese version of the text by Hsüan-tsang, it is said : this text belongs to the *Sarvāstivāda* school'.

The *Saṅgītiparyāya* is divided into twelve section :

1. *Nidāna* (introduction) concerning compilation of othe text and such other matters; 2. One *dharma*-all beings live on food etc. ; 3. Two *dharmas*-mind and matter etc.; 4. Three *dharmas*-three roots of bad and good etc.' 5. Four *dharmas*-four Applications of mindfulness (*smṛtyupasthāna*), four noble Truths etc. ; 6. Five *dharmas*-five (*skandhas*) etc. 7. Six *dharmas*-

six *vedanākāya* etc.; 8. Seven *dharmas*-seven Factors of enlightenment, seven latent tendencies (*anuśaya*) etc.; 9. Eight *dharmas*-Eight-fold pàth, eight *pudgalas* etc. ; 10. Nine *dharmas*-nine abodes of being (*sattvāvāsa*) etc.; 11. Ten *dharmas*-ten objects of mystic meditation (*krtsnāyatana*) etc. 12. Concluding Chapter on the Buddha's admonition to the *bhikṣus* to read and recite the *Saṅgītiparyāya* as collected at the Council.

Takakusu mentions that the *Saṅgitiparyāya* quotes the *Dharmaskandha*[10] while Poussin observes that the *Prajnāptiśāstra* refers to the *Saṅgītiparyāya.*[11]

The Chinese version of the *Dharmaskandhapādaśāstra*, i.e., the *A p'i ta mo fa yun tsu lun by* Hsüan-tsang in 659 A.D. is available in *T.* 26, No. 1537. The original text that is lost, is attributed to Sāriputra by Yasomitra and in Chinese tradition to Mahāmaudgalyāyana (*Ta mu chien lien*). According to Prof. Nakamura, the originaltext of the *Dharmaskandha* was probably composed 400 years after the *parinirvāṇa* of the Buddha.[12] Sanskrit fragments of the text have been found and studied.[13] The text in its Chinese translation is arranged in 12 fasciculi (*chüan*) and 21 chapters. At the end of each *chuan*, the text is mentioned as belonging to the *Sarvāstivāda* school.

All important aspects of the fundamental principles of the *Sarvāstivāda* school are detailed in the *Dharmaskandha*, In general, the text outlines the course of spiritual training of a Buddhist monk. N.Dutt. holds that the text may be parallaled to the *Viśuddhimagga* of Buddhaghosa.[14]

The *Dharmaskandha* deals with the following topics in its 21 chapters :

1. Five precepts (*śila*); 2. Four Attainments leading to the first stage of the Buddhist disciple (*srotāpatyaṅga*); 3. Four Attainments of faith and purity ; 4. Four Fruits of religious life *śrāmaṇyaphala* 5. Four modes of progress to deliverance ; 6.

Four classes of the Buddha's disciples ; 7. Four right strivings. 8. Four Application of mindfulness ; 10. Four Noble Truths ; 11. Four Meditative absorptions ; 12. Four Immesurables ; 13. Four formless spheres ; 14. Four cultivations of Absorptions , 15. Seven factors of enlightement 16. Miscelleneous mattters that deal with 78 types of defilments ; 17, Twenty two controlling Faculties ; 18. Twelve Bases ; 19. Five Aggregates ; 20. various Elements ; 21. Dependent origination.

The text quotes a lot from the *sūtras.* In fact, excepting the chapters onthe *indriyas* and miscelleneous matters (i.e., chapter 17 and 1,6) all others are said to been taken from the *sūtras* (Pruden : xiviii)

The Chinese version of the *Vijñānakāyapādaśāstra*, i.e. the *A p'i ta mo shih shen tsu lun*, by Hsüan -tsang (649 A.D.) exists in *T.*26, no. 1539. The original text is attributed to Devaśarmā (Ti-po she mo) in Chinese tradition that says that the text was composed 100 years after the *parinirvāṇa* of the Buddha, at Viśoka near Śrāvasti. According to Takakausu, *Vijñānakāya* means the 'Body or group of (subjects connected with) consciousness-although it appears to be employed differently in its technical sense.[15]

The *Vijñānakāya* in its Chinese version is divided into six groups (*yün*) and sixteen fasciculi (*chuan*). At the end of *chuan* 1, 2,4,5,and 7-10, it is mentioned that the text belongs to the *Sarvāstivāda* school. Group one entitled *Mu chien lien yun* (*Maudgalyāyana*) contains expositions on *pudgala, indriya, citta, kleśa, Vijñāna* etc., as given by Maudgalyāyana and also the refutation of his opinion on the existence of the past and the future. The second group entitled Pu tu chieh lo(*pudgala*) discusses theory of *pudgala* and its relation to the theory of knowledge. The Third group, i.e. *Yin Yuan Yuan* (*Hetupratyaya*) defines the functions of mental states as *hetu* (cause). Group four entitled *Suo Yuan* (*Ālambanapratyaya*) defines the same as *ālambana* (basis) and deals with various problems of cognition in the past, present and future. The fifth group,i.e. *Tsa Yun* (*Miscellaneous*) and the sixth group, i.e. *Cheng Chiu* (*Samanvāgama*, enumerates mental states of a person under training and of the *arhat* (the perfect one).

The Sanskrit original of the *Abhidharma-Dhātukāya-pādaśātra* is lost and is preserved in its Chines e version (title A *p'i ta mo chieh shen tsu lun,* T. No. 1540) - by Hsüan -tsang in 663 A.D. At the end of its three main divisions or *chuans*, the text is mentioned as belonging to the *Sarvāstivāda* school. Hsuan-tsang mentions the Chinese name of the *Dhātukāya* among the six supplementary texts of *Abhidharma.* The Chinese name of the *Dhātukāya* also appears in a colophon by K'uei chi, another disciple of Hsüan tsang as one the six *pāda* works to the *Jñānaprasthāna* which belongs tothe *Sarvāstivāda* school. It is also mentioned that the original text of the *Dhatukāya* was composed by the venerable Shi-yu (Vasumitra).[16] However, accordiong to Yaśomitra (*Sphutārthā, AK.*1.3) and Bu-ston, Purṇa was author of the text.

In the title *Abhidharma-Dhātukāya-pādaśāstra*, the word *dhātu* (element) refers to all mental faculties or attributes which are considered as seperate elements in the *Abhidharma* tradition. Thus *Dhātukāya* means groups of attributes which constitute mind itself.

The text is divided into two Chapters. In the first Chapter, the functions of the mind are classified as the enumeration of subjects,i.e. the ten *mahābhūmikadharmas*, theten *kleśamahābhūmikadharmas*, the ten *upakleśamahā-bhūmikadharmas*, the five *kleśas*, the five *dṛṣṭis*, the five *sparśas*, the five *indriyas*, the five *dharmas*, the six *vijñānakāyas*, the six *cetanākāyas*, and the six *tṛṣṇākāyas.* In the second chapter of the *Dhātukāya*, the mutual relation of the mental states are discussed.

The *Abhidharma-Prakaraṇapāda -śāstra* is preserved in two Chinese translations, one by Guṇabhadra and Bodhiyaśas (435-

443 A.D.), and the other by Hsüan-tsang (659 A.D.). The latter version entitled *A p'i ta mo p'in lei tsu lun* (hereafter *APPS*) is available in *T*,vol.26, pp.690 b -777a 20). According to the scholars , in the oldest Chinese versionof the text made inthe middle of the second century A.D. , three chapters were separately translated of which two arestill extant. Moreover, a commentary tothe first Chapter was composed by Dharmatrāta in the fourth century and was also translated into Chinese. Sanskrit fragments of the *APPS* are quoted in the AKV (7;11.46, 54; Vll, 44 etc).

The original *APPS* is attributed to the venerable Vasumitra, the famous *Sarvāstivāda* master wholived two or three hundred years afterthe *parinirvāna* of the Buddha. Hsüan-tsang says that Vasumitra wrote the *Dhātukāya* (another *pāda* work) and the *Prakarṇapāda* near Puṣkarāvatī in Gandhara.

Professor Warder holds that Vasumitra I, probably in 100 B.C. enlarged the *Dhātukāya* (one of the seven *śāstras* belonging to an early date) with discusion on *dharmas*,their definitions and classifications and composed the *APPS* which is the last of the seven *Abhidharmaśāstras* of the *Sarvāstivāda*. However, Poussin inhis introduction to the *Abhidharma-Kośa-Bhāṣysaṃ* maintains that the *APPS* is earlier thanthe *Jñānaprasthāna-śāstra* as the former ignores the *akuśalamahābhūmika* category accepted by the latter. The *Vibhāsā* seems to be unsure onthe question as to whether the *APPS* or the *Jñānaprasthāna* is the earlier.

The *APPS* contains eight sections with 18 fasciculi. The contents of the text will be analysed in a separate chapter. In brief, the first section is devoted to the enumeration of the five *dharmas-rūpa, citta, caitta, cittaviprayukta* and *asaṃskṛta*. The second section explains the ten knowledge, which are identical with those of the fourth and the fifth chapters of the third book of the *Jñānaprasthāna*. The third section deals with the attainments of the knowledge of the organs of the senses and their objects. The Fourth Section explains the seven categories, i.e., Elements, Bases, groups, Basic mind states, pure mental states, Defiled mental states, and Minor Defiled states. In its fifth section, the *APPS* deals with the ninety-eight latent tendencies (*anuśaya*) that tend to become conditions for the arising of ever new defilements. Section six gives an exposition of the *dharmas* that can be inferred and such other matters. One thousand questions on various ethical and meditational practices of Buddhism are discussed in the seventh section of the text. The Eighth Section is a résumé of the issues discussed in the entire text. As the eight sections are independent of each other, the *Prakaraṇapāda* is considered as a collection of eight works.

Scholars like B.C. Law holds that the *APPS* agrees to a large extent with the *Vibhaṅgrprakaraṇa* of the *Abhidhammapitaka* of the *Sthaviravādins*. He further claims that the text is probably a counter part of an earlier compilation of the *Suttānta-bhājaniya* part of the *Vibhaṅga.*[17]

The *Prajñapatiśāstra* is one of the six *pāda* works belonging probably to an earlier period. The text is lost in its original and is preserved in Chinese and in Tibetan. The subject matter of the text is drawn from popular beliefs on the world of gods, demons, etc. but it quotes from the *Āgamas* and explains the same in *ābhidharmic* style. Sanskrit fragments in the *AKV* (I.37; II.45; VII.40) are identified with those of the *Prajñaptiśāstra.*

The Chinese version of the *Prajnaptiśāstra*, i.e., the *shih she lun* exists in an incomplete Chinese translation (T.26,1538) and in a Tibetan translation. The original text is attributed to Maudgalyāyana and was translated around 1055 A.D. by Fa-hu (Dharmapāla or Dharmarakṣā). In Tibetan version, three sections of the text, i.e., *lokaprajñapti*, *kāranaprajñapti* and *karma prajñapti* are available. The Chinese translation has only the second section in addition to twelve other sections. In the *lokaprajñapti* the cosmological ideas of the Buddhist are given whereas in the *kāranaprajñapti*, the characteristics of a *Bodhisattva* is discussed. In the *karmaprajñapti*, different kinds of deeds are enumerated and classified. Other topics discused in the text include seven *ratnas* of a *cakravarti* kings, thirty-two *mahāpurusa lakṣaṇas*, moral defilements, i.e., *rāga*, *dveṣa* and *moha*, *tṛṣṇā*, drowsines, arrogance etc. and their causes, difference between mental faculties of the Buddha and his disciples, 32 signs of the Buddha, eight causes of rain etc. According to B.C. Law this text resembles the *Lakkhana Suttānta* of the *D*.III.[18]

2. Fundamental *Abhidharma*

The *Abhidharma* is largely devoted to the discussion of the *dharma* or the teachings of the *Nikāyas* and the *Agamas*. The *Ābhidharmic* sources before the fundamental *Abhidharma* deal with thirty items concerning the teaching which have been mentioned elsewhere.[19] In general, those items treat on knowledge, wrong view, mindfulness, controlling faculties, sphere of existence, action, path, truth, insight, factors of enlightenment, psychic power, behaviour (*caryā*) etc. These important topics were arranged, elaborated and organised in the *Sarvāstivāda Abhidharma* texts like the *Dharmaskandha*, the *Saṅgitiparyāya*, the *Prajñaptiśāstra* etc. Besides the doctrinal items, worldly problems on cause, action, world etc. are also analysed as may be found in the *Prajnaptiśāstra*. The emphasis of all those texts, however, was on the practices of Buddhism.

Prof. Warder observes (p. 82) that the set of the seven topics on the thirty seven *bodhipakṣīya dharmas* probably constitute the earliest form of *Abhidharma*. In the compilation of the *Dharmaskandha*, 'a dozen or more headings were added' to each of the seven topics. These headings include five Groups (*śkandha*), twelve Bases (*āyatana*) and eighteen Elements (*dhātu*) besides the Four truths (*āryasatya*), conditions (*pratyaya*), four Meditations (*samādhi*) and some other topics.[20] The later fundamental *Abhidharma* applied new theories to the items of early Buddhism for the establishment of the sectarian views. Thus the contents came to be studied as a whole and in an objective manner.

The analytical study of the *skandha, āyatana* and *dhātu* is established in the fundamental *Abhidharma* to classify those *dharmas* into the principles of matter (*rūpa*) and mind (*nāma*), or to explain them from philosophical and psychological viewpoints. This marks the first stage of the development of *Abhidharma* philosophy. Theories concerning the nature of *dharma* as momentery phenomena constantly changing but causally connected with succesive moments rejected the concepts of self or personality (*pudgala*) or substantiality of being in either material or immaterial. Besides, religious contents like the Buddha's superior personality and his various attributes and epithets (*Bhagavān* etc) are also available in the *Dharmaskandha* and the *Prajnaptipādaśāstra.* A detailed treatment on the attainments of the *upāsakas* (lay adherents) is also made in the first text.

The texts of the *Sarvāstivāda Abhidharma* like the *Vijñānakāya*, the *Dhātukāya* etc. demonstrate their distinguishing characters by asserting the *Sarvāstivāda* doctrines. The first text establishes the cardinal principle of the sect on the real existence of the *dharma* (phenomena) in the past, present and future. It also explains the four conditions (*pratyaya*) in detail. Mental states are defined and analysed with classification in the *Dhātukāya.*

With this concentration on the theories, the study of *Abhidharma* became isolated from the practice, resulting in the emergence of the classification and categorisation of the contents. This is clearly expressed in the texts like the *Prakaranapāda*, part of the *Dhātukāya*, and the *Jñānaprasthāna*, All the subjects treated in the earlier texts of *Abhidharma* were treated deeply with their broader implications in those three texts that brought the completion of the fundamental *Abhidharma.* This will be detailed lateron. In short, Fundamental *Abhidharma* gradually came to underline in particular the contents of its own.

Broadly speaking, *Abhidharma* is an analysis and methodological elaboration of what was already given in the Buddha's discourses. Fundamental *Abhidharma* in particular demonstrates the following methods- (a) new classification of contents by categories, (b) various doctrines are arranged in numerical order, or in a systematic maner, (c) exposition of doctrines with more clear definitions and detailed terminology, (d) explanation of topics (e) methods of exposition by-(i) questioning with arangement into various branches (*praśnapṛcchā* or *pañhāpucchā*), (ii) Conjunctions (*saṃyukta*), and inclusion into classes (*saṃgraha*) of the objects of discourses and (iii) association (*saṃprayoga*) and dissociation (*viprayoga*) of various mental categories.

In the fundamental *abhidharma* text of the *APPS*, all forms of existence were clasified into five categories,i.e. *rūpa* (matter), *citta* (mind), *caitta*, (mental attribute) *cittaviprayukta dharma* (*dharmas* nor associated with the mind), and *asaṃskṛtadharma* (Non-created). Earlier *nāma-rūpa* (mind and matter) were classified by categories as five *skandhas*, twelve *āyatanas* and eighteen *dhātus.* The new classification was more objective and adequate. In the *Dharmaskandha* various doctrines from *pañcaśīla* (*wu-chiai*) to *dvādaśanidāna pratityasamutpāda* (*yuan-chi*) are arranged in a systematic manner. So far asthe elaboration of topics is concerned, the topics of the thirty-seven *bodhipakṣīya dharmas*, considered as the summary of the teachings of the Buddha are also elaborated in the text. The *Saṇgītiparyāya* arranged the subjects of the Buddha's discourses in numerical order from one to ten and is a developed form of the *Saṅgītisutta.* The seven texts of the fundamental *Abhidharma* emphasized onthe accuracy of the definitions which are also more clear than the older definitions which were kinds of lists of equivalent terms derived from same linguistic roots.

For explanation of the important items, some texts like the *Dharmaskandha* quotes and explains the early *Āgama* texts while some of them like the *Prakaranapādaśāstra* treat the topics independently following various *Ābhidharmic* methods. To illustrate, the classification of teaching by ' Questioning' is done on the basis of 22 triplets (*tika*) and 100 doublets (*duka*) which are considered as ' standards of consideration.' In *Sthaviravāda* tradition, the list of 22 *tikas* and 100 *dukas* at the beginning of the Pali *Dhammasaṅgaṇi* is the basis of that book. Other Pāli Fundamental *Abhidhamma* texts have also analysed the *dhammas* accordiong to those *tikas* and *dukas.* This has been treated elsewhere (Watanabe, pp.47-53). In the *Sarvāstivāda Abhidharma* text of the *Prakaraṇapāda* (pp.696b15-698 a 27), twelve *āyatanas* are analysed by adding 28 doublets and four triplets. Doublets are used in the same text to analyses other *dharmas,* specially *anuśaya* (*sui-mien*). The *Dhātukāya-pādśāstra* treats mental categories under the three classes of elements (*dhātu*), bases (*āyatana*), and aggregates (*skandha*). Then text further enumerates the relations of the above categories in terms of inclusion,exclusin, association and dissociation of the same. This has been detailed in my study elsewhere.[21]

3. Compilation of the seven texts

The seven *Sarvāstivāda Abhidharma* texts (Ch.I,8) that comprise the *Sarvāstivāda Abhidharma Piṭaka* are known as the fundamental *Abhidharma* texts of the *Sarvāstivādins.* From the viewpoint of the development of the *Abhidharma* in the *Sarvāstivāda* tradition, these texts i.e. the *Jñānaprasthāna etc,* refer to the 'compilation (*piṇḍīkṛtya,* Chinese *chieh-chi*) of the

Ābhidhārmic elements found in the *āgamas* or the discourse of the Buddha.[22]

The period of the compilation of the fundamental texts of the *Sarvāstivada Abhidharma* is assigned by the scholars to extend from about the middle of the 3rd century B.C. to the beginning of the Christian era.[23] This period witnessed the separation of various sects of Buddhism covering the process of the first branching as well as the final sub-branching.[24] Presumably, the compilations of the *Abhidharma* texts by each sect were also finalized during this period. So far as the fundamental *Sarvāstivāda Abhidharma* texts are concerned, one is amazed with the enormous growth of thought and doctrines in those texts. Hence the compilation of those texts must have taken a considerable time for their production. With regard to subject-matter and methodology, the fundamental *Abhidharma* texts show a gradual divergence of the sectarian *Abhidharma of the Sarvāstivāda* from the original *Abhidharma* traceable in the *Sūtra* and the *Vinaya.*

With regard to the seven texts in Chinese, three stages of the growth of the fundamental *Abhidharma* may be specially distinguished:

1. Early or original *Abhidharma* of the *Sarvāstivādins* represented by the *Saṅgītiparyāya,* the *Dharmaskandha* and the *Prajñaptiśāstra.*

2. *Abhidharma* of the middle period represented by the *Vijñānakāya* and the *Dhātukāya.*

3. *Abhidharma* of the late period represented by the *Prakaraṇapāda* and the *Jñānaprasthāna.*

The seven *abhidharma* texts comprising the *Abhidharma Piṭaka* of the *Sthaviravādins* mentioned earlier are also considered as the productions of the development of fundamental *Abhidharma* in the three stages.

Early *Sarvāstivāda Abhidharma* Texts

Early *Abhidharma* developed as the explanation of the *sūtras*. But the immediate disciples of the Buddha, i.e., Sāriputra, Maudgalyāyana and Mahākausṭhila or Kātyāyana carried out the discourses on those explanations to a full sense of discussion on the doctrines so as to systematise the same. In the later phases of the development of the *Abhidharma* by the different sects, it became dissociated from the *sūtras* and new doctrines emerged within it. Gradually the sects, which resembled each other in earlier phase, displayed great differences of opinions that became evident in the doctrinal contents, methods and forms of the *Abhidharma* as the last collection of the Buddhist canon. So far as the seven *Abhidharma* texts of the *Sarvāstivāda* are concerned, the *Saṅgītiparyāya*, the *Dharmaskandha*, and the *Prajñaptiśāstra* demonstrate the characteristics of early *Abhidharma*.

The text of the *Saṅgītiparyāya* is considered as the earliest *abhidharma* of the *Sarvāstivāda*. It explains the *dharmas* mainly by quoting the *sūtras*. Warder considers the text as an 'enormous *mātṛkā*' that presents list of *dharmas* in more than two hundred headings (p. 220). Dr. B.C. Law places the *Saṅgītiparyāya* before the Pāli *Saṅgītisuttānta*.[25]

As mentioned earlier, the doctrinal contents of the text constitute of the practical teaching (on *śīla* and *samādhi*) of the Buddha, explained by *sūtra* quotations, with more than two hundred headings arranged in a numerical order in the manner of the *Saṅgītisūtra*. A large number of Buddhist technical terms are collected in the text with minute details and definitions in typical *ābhidhārmic* style. The purpose is to distinguish the *dharma* as arranged in the *Saṅgītisūtra* and elaborate them. In this sense, the *Sañgītiparyāya* may be regarded as a commentary on the *Saṅgītisūtra*.

The method of *abhidharma* adopted by the *Saṅgītiparyāya* is '*sūtra*-analysis' which is *apraśnaka*[26] 'without questions' (detailed earlier). The method of argument in the text has been discussed elsewhere.

The *Dharmaskandha* that deals with groups of *dharma* (*dharmaskandha*) is considered as the development of the *Chachakka-sūtra* in which Buddha's teaching were elaborated by his disciples with the method of grouping of the doctrinal topics (*mātikā*). The arrangement of the *mātikās* in groups was the early system of *Abhidharma* (see p. 8). The groups of doctrinal topics or *mātikās* have been classified as (1) the doctrines of the Buddha which are to be practised, i.e., the thirty-seven *bodhipaksīya dharmas* and (2) the teaching of *pratītyasamutpāda* etc, the philosophical understanding of which leads to enlightenment. The *Dharmaskandha* demonstrates a system of arranging all the *dharmas* of the two groups, a characteristically *Ābhidhārmic* system which is only anticipated and not explicit inthe *Nikāyas* and the *Āgamas.*

The first fifteen chapters of the text elaborate the ethical doctrines leading to enlightement and the rest explain the theoretical doctrines related to insight. In the first three chapters many doctrines are included which are to be studied by the laymen and the novices of the Buddha's path. Next three chapters (4-6) discuss the methods of studying Buddhism, The last nine chapters (7-17) explain the thirty-seven *dharmas* and other practices. Thus the grouping of the topics in the text is clearly an attempt to arrange the doctrines of the Buddha following a definite system. Four meditations and four immeasurables (*apramāna)* are explained in the eleventh and the twelfth chapters of the text. The lowest meditation starts from the four meditations and the highest meditation is arranged in the four immeasurables. Thus both the *dharmas* are related to eachother. In short, the text arranges and explains all the important topics discussed in the six other texts of the fundamental *Abhidharma* composed not earlier to it. Admittedly the text may be regarded as the original text of the *Sarvāstivāda Abhidharma.*

The *Prajñaptiśāstra,* as we have mentioned earlier, deals with *loka* (world), *karma* (action), and *hetu* (causes) from worldly standpoints. The Chinese version of the text preserves only the *hetu-prajñapti* which describes in its first section the causes of the seven treasures,i.e. *Strī, gṛhapati, parināyaka, cakra, hastin, aśva* and *maṇi* of the *cakravartirāja* (universal king). In other 11 sections, the text deals with 'temporal issues' like the signs of the Buddha; causes of physical world, of various mental and physical phenomena; and other popular subjects.[27] These items were mentioned briefly in the *Nikāyas* and *Āgamas.* The original teachings of the Buddha are thus unified with the worldly objects in the early phase of the fundamental *Abhidharma.* In addition to this, the text quotes many *sūtras* from the *Āgamas* which is one of the characteristics of early *Abhidharma.*

Abhidharma texts of the middle period :

The early fundamental *Abhidharma* texts ofthe *Sarvāstivāda* tradition has many similarities with the Pāli *Abhidharma* texts. From the view point of subject matter and methodology the *Dharmaskandha* and the *Prajñaptiśāstra* may be compared with the *Vibhaṅga* and the *Puggala-paññatti.*[28] The *Vijñānakāya* and the *Dhātukāya* are considered as the fundamental *Abhidharma* texts belonging to the middle period since the texts demonstrate distinctive *Sarvāstivāda* feature which are not available inthe Pāli *Abhidharma* texts. The *Vijñānakāya* particularly establishes two *Sarvāstivāda* theories of 1) the existence of *dharmas* in the past, present and future, and 2) non-ego (*anātmā).* In the first sections of the text, Maudgalyāyana's position on the reality of the present is refuted and in the second sections the idea of 'everlasting entity' is rejected with the refutation of the existence of *Pudgala* (personality), with arguments from the viewpoints of the *Sarvāstivādins.*

The text in its third and fourth section introduces the theory of four *pratyayas* (*yüan*, condition) i.e. *hetupratyaya* (cause as condition), *ālambanapratyaya* (object as condition), *samanantarapratyaya* (immediate condition) and *adhipatipratyaya* (predominance condition).

The *Dhātukāya* is a systematic treatment on *ābhidhārmic* definitions, terminology and classification. The text is divided into three chapters. The first chapter is devoted to the enumerations and definitions of the mental attributes. After the enumeration of subjects, the *Dhātukāya* defines the items in the list. The definitions are developed from the early *ābhidhārmic* style, as seen in the *Dhammasaṅgaṇi* and in the *Vibhaṅga.* They consist of synonymous terms to clarify the concepts regarding particular terms. The classification of the thirty *Mahābhūmikadharmas* appear for the the first time in the *abhidharma.*

The second chapter deals with the association and dissociation, inclusion and exclusions of the above attributes which are again grouped into the three categories of 18 elements, 12 bases and 5 aggregates. These attributes are explained in Pāli *Abhidhamma* texts like the *Dhammasaṅgaṇi,* the *Vibhaṅga,* and the *Dhātukathā,* and in the *Sarvāstivāda Abhidharma* texts the *Jñānaprasthana,* the *Prakaraṇapāda,* and the *Vijñānakāya.* However, the *dhātus* are exclusively treated only in the *Dhātukāya.* Although the text has some striking similarities with the *Dhātukathā* in the treatment of the classification of the mental states, yet the details of the characteristics of the functions of the states are not detailed inthe manner of the *Dhātukāya,* that provides systematic and complete informations about the *dhātus* or mental attributes. This was done probably to safeguard the doctrines from sectarian innovations.

In the second chapter of the *Dhātukāya,* the mutual relations of the mental attributes are discussed. These are treated under the three categories of elements, bases, and aggregates. In each of the sixteen sections, a mental state of enquiry is paired with the category next in order. In the first three sections the states of inquiryare examined with reference to the nature and mutual relations of the mental states in terms of association (*samprayoga*) and dissociation (*viprayoga*). The co-existence of the mind states and their attributes are considered as *samprayoga.* The detachment of the mind states from the attributes are considered as *viprayoga.* The classification done this way was completed later in the *Prakaraṇa-pāda.*

Late *Sarvāstivāda Abhidharma* Texts :.

The *Prakaranapādaśātra* and the *Jñānaprasthāna* are considered as belonging to the late period of fundamental *Abhidharma* of the *Sarvāstivādins.* In its first chapter the *Prakaraṇa* makes a systematic classification of phenomena into *rūpa, citta, caitta, cittaviprayukta* and *asaṃskṛta,* which is more objective than earlier classification of things into five *skandha,* twelve *āyatana* and eighteen *dhātu.* Next ten forms of knowledge are explained with respect to their differentiation, result, their inclusion in one another etc. The classification of 12 *āyatanas,* 18 *dhātus* and 5 *skandhas* is detailed through the method of 'questioning' (*Praśnapṛcchā*). The description of the items from the *mahābhūmika-dharmas* to the six *tṛṣṇākāyas* is similar to that of the *Dhātukaya,* whereas they are forty in the *Prakaraṇapāda.*

A new classification of the *anuśayas* into ninety eight groups also appear in the text. Besides, the Buddhist practices from the *śikṣāpadas* to different *dhyānas* are comprehensively treated in the same. In short, the *Prakaraṇapāda* may be regarded as a complete text of othe fundamental *Abhidharma* of the *Sarvāstivādins,* The *Jñānaprasṭhana* is known as the basic text that deals with the *Ābhidhārmic* topics as a whole while the six other fundamental texts deal them separately. The doctrines of *samyojana, Jñāna, karuṇā, mahābhūta, indriya, samādhi* and *dṛṣṭi* described in its eight chapters are expressed in difficult technical terms. In the beginning of every chapters a series of questions are asked and answered. Then they are treated one by one. The structure of the text is very loose and the ideas are hard to understand for ordinary people. Thus the text demonstrates a developed form of fundamental *Abhidharma* which has few similarities with early phases of the same.

NOTES

1 *Vibhāṣa.* P.236b (details in English by Pruden from French version of Poussin in the *Abhidharma koṣabhāṣyam, op.cit.*,pp.18-20. For *AKB,* see f.n.I.

2 Pruden, *ibid.,* p.17.

3 Takakusu,*op.cit.,* p.84.

4 Pruden, *op.cit.*,p.17

5 Among the eight chapters of the Chinese translation by Saṅghadeva, first two have been retranslated into Sanskrit by Santibhiksu Sastri (Visva Bharati, Vol.I., Santiniketan,1955). The whole text has been translated into Japanese by G.Nishi and Y. Sakamato.

6 Takakusu, *op. cit.* p. 84

7 Sanskrit fragments of the *Saṅgīti-pāryāya* have been published in Waldschmidt, *Sanskrithandschrithandschriften aus den Turfanfunden; in Das Sangitisutra and sein Kommnetar Sangītiparyāya;* and an *Das Pañcavastukam and die Pañca-vastukavibhāṣā.*

8 Takakusu, *op. cit.,* p. 100.

9 See Poussin's introduction translated into English by Pruden, *Op. cit.,* p. 28.

10 Takakusu, *Op. cit.,* p. 112.

11 Pruden, *Op. cit.*, p. 28.

12 Nakamura, *Op. cit.*, p. 106.

13 Takasaki, "Remarks on the Sanskrit Fragment of the *Abhidharma Dharmaskandhapāda-śāstra*" in *Journal of Indian and Buddhist Studies*, 13, 1965, pp. 33-41; and *Dharma-skandha*, edited by Siglinde Dietz in *Fragmente des Dharmaskandha: ein Abhidharma - Text in Sanskrit aus Gilgit*, 1984.

14 N. Dutt, Buddhist sects in India; *Op. cit.* P. 146.

15 Takakusu, *Op, cit.* p. 107.

16 *Ibid.* p. 109.

17 B.C. Law, *History of Pali literature*, p. 340.

18 *Ibid.* p. 342.

19 See my article "Origin of *Abhidharma*".

20 Warder, *Op. cit.* p. 221.

21 Swati Ganguly, *Op. cit.*, pp. 51&109.

22 Cf, AKB, P. 15 - *śāstrā kila Buddhhienābhidharma uktaḥ; satu prakīrña ukto Bhagavatā, Bhadantakātyāyanīputrapravṛtibhiḥ piṇḍīkṛtya sthāpitaḥ.*

23 Hirakawa, *Op.* cit p. 131; Banerjee, *Op. cit.*, P. 69-70; Nakamura, *Op. cit.;* p. 105 n. 18.

24 For details, see Masuda, Jiryo, "Origin and Doctrines of Early Indian Buddhist Schools" in *Asia Major*, 2, 1925 pp. 1-78, being an English translation of Hsüan-Tsang's Chinese rendering (*Taisho* 203) of the *Samayabhedoparacana cakra.* For a comprehensive account, see Hirakawa, *ibid*, pp. 107-116.

[25] B.C. Law, *Op. cit.*, P. 339.

[26] Watanabe, *Op. cit.*, p. 92.

[27] Details in Encyclopaedia, *Op. cit.*, p. 70.

[28] Watanabe, *Op. cit.*, p. 62-63.

EARLY *ABHIDHARMA* PHILOSOPHY AND PRACTICES : AN ANALYSIS OF THE *A-P'I-TA-MO-FA-YUN-TSU-LUN* (*ABHIDHARMA-DHARMASKANDHA-PĀDA ŚĀSTRA*)

Prelude

Broadly speaking, *Abhidharma-Dharmaskandha-pādaśāstra* (hereafter *ADSPS*) comprises the various stages of an adept in Buddhist Path along with some important doctrines of the Buddhist philosophy. The Path (*magga* or *mārga*) stands for two kinds of path:—

1. The four supramundane (*lokottara*) paths, i.e. the stages of the adept, *śrotāpanna, sakṛdāgāmi, anāgāmi* and *arhat.*

2. The Eightfold Path (*aṣṭāṅgika mārga*) leading to extinction of suffering (*duḥkhanirodha*), i.e., Right View, Right Thought, Right Speech, Right Bodily Action, Right Livelihood, Right Effort, Right Mindfulness and Right Concentration.

In the Buddhist tradition, the first kind of Path refers to the various stages of progress attained by an adept while the *Aṣṭāṅgika mārga* refers to the training (*śikṣā*) and attainments of an adept during the various stages of progress by complying with the rules of *śīla* (moral precepts), rules of *samādhi*, (concentration) and the rules of *prajñā* (Wisdom). Thus Right Speech, Right Bodily Action and Right Livelihood are the Paths attained by moral training; Right Effort, Right Mindfulness, and Right Concentration are the Paths attained by *samādhi*; Right View and Right Thought are the Paths attained by complying with the rules of Wisdom.

In the present study the contents of the first 16 sections of the *ADSPS* comprised of the various stages of progress of an adept in the Buddhist Path have been arranged under two heads:-

Instructions and Faith (Chapters 1 - 6, on *śīla*),

Practice and Enlightenment (7 - 15, on *samādhi* and *prajñā*)

On the other hand, Chapters 17 - 21 of the *ADSPS* contain miscellaneous subjects including some important doctrines of Buddhist philosophy like *skandha* etc. and those doctrines have been arranged under the following head :

Essentials of Buddhist Philosophy.

The analysis of the contents of the *ADSPS* in the light of those three topics aims at a comprehensive understanding of the subject of the *ADSPS.* Finally a comparison of the Chinese text of the *ADSPS* with relevant Buddhist texts in Pāli and Sanskrit may help to explore some similarities in the expositions of the early Buddhist teachings preserved in the original texts in Chinese, Pāli and Sanskrit.

1. DETAILED CONTENTS OF THE CHINESE *ADSPS*

Chapter - I Precepts (*śikṣāpadāni*), on the attainments by the *upāsakas*.

Introductory *śloka*

Chinese Text

The Buddha's instruction on the Five Precepts 453 C6 - 9

Five misconducts, i.e. *prāṇātipāta, adattādāna,*
453 C10-454a14

'Abstaining from taking life for lifetime'

What is 'one who takes life'

What is 'taking life'

What is 'being violent'

What is 'blood-stained hand' etc.

'Abstaining from taking what is not given' 456 a3 - b2

What is 'one who takes what is not given' etc.

'Abstaining from False speech for lifetime' 457 b22 - c27

What is 'one who speaks lie' etc.

'Abstaining from the use of intoxicants that cause indolence for lifetime' 457 c28 - 458 a 17

What is one who uses intoxicants that cause indolence' etc.

What is 'instruction' (*śikṣā*) 458 a18 - 22

What is 'step' (*pada*)

Attainments of *bhikṣu, bhikṣuṇi, śikṣamā*ṇa, 458 a 23 - b 19

śikṣamāṇā, and *upāsaka.*

Chapter - II Conditions of Attaining The stream

(*srotāpatyaṅgāṇi*)

Chinese Text

The Buddha's instruction on *srotāpatyaṅgas* 458 b 26 - 28

Four *srotāpatyaṅgas* 458 b 28 - c[illegible]

'Companionship with good persons' 458 c8 - 28

Chapter - III Attainments of Faith and Purity (*avetyaprasāda*)

Chinese Text

Chapter - IV Attainments of Fruits of Religious Life (*śrāmaṇyaphalāni*)

Attainment of conditioned *srotāpattiphala* 464 c 24 - 26

Attainment of unconditioned *srotāpattiphala*464 c 27 - 465 a1

Attainment of conditioned *sakṛdāgāmiphala* 465 a 2 - 5

Attainment of unconditioned *sakṛdāgāmiphala* 465 a 2 - 5

Attainment of conditioned *anāgāmiphala* 465 a 6 - 9

Attainment of unconditioned *anāgāmiphala* 465 a 9 - 12

Attainment of conditioned *arhatvaphala* 465 a 13 - 17

Attainment of unconditioned *arhatvaphala* 465 a 17 - 21

Chapter - V Ways to Knowledge (*abhijñāpratipad*)

Chinese Text

The Buddha's instruction on *abhijñāpratipad* 465 a 23 - 24

Four modes of progress in following the way to deliverance 465 a 25

What is (1) painful progress with slow comprehension 465 a 26 - b 19

What is (2) painful progress with quick comprehension 465 b 19 - c 11

What is (3) pleasant progress with slow comprehension 465 c 12 - 466

What is (4) pleasant progress with quick comprehension 466 a 13 - b 8

Attainments in the four modes of progress 466 b 9 - 14

Chapter - VI Noble Lineage (*āryavaṃśa*)

Chapter - VII Right Striving (*samyakpradhāna*)

Attainments of striving to abandon *kāmacchanda nīvaraṇa* and other *nīvaraṇas* that has arisen

As to 'one who strives for non-arising of 469 a 12 - 470 a 14 bad unwholesome *dharmas* that may arise in future', what are 'bad unwholesome *dharmas* that may arise in future' What is non-arising of *kāmacchanda-nīvaraṇa* that may arise in future'

Attainments of striving for non-arising of *kāmacchanda nīvaraṇa* and other *nīvaraṇas* that may arise in future.

As to 'one who strives for arising of good 470a15-17 wholesome *dharmas* that have not arisen', what are good wholesome *dharmas* that have not arisen, four stages of meditation and the three formless stages

Arising of good wholesome *dharmas* in the first meditation 470a18-b4

Arising of good wholesome *dharmas* in the second 470b5 meditation

Arising of good wholesome *dharmas* in the third 470b6-c13 meditation

Arising of good wholesome *dharmas* in the fourth 470c14-15 meditation

As to 'one who strives to maintain, 470c16 cultivate and to increase the good wholesome *dharmas* that have arisen', what are good wholesome *dharmas* that have arisen

Striving to cultivate etc. the good wholesome 470c17-471a9 *dharmas* that have arisen in the first meditation

Striving to cultivate etc. the good wholesome 471a9 *dharmas* that have arisen in the second meditation

Striving to cultivate etc. the good wholesome 471a10-29 *dharmas* that have arisen in the third meditation

Striving to cultivate good wholesome *dharmas*that 471b1-26

have arisen in the fourth meditation

On the name of 'right striving' 471b26-c11

Chapter-VIII Bases of power (*ṛddhipāda*)

Chinese Text

The Buddha's instruction on *ṛddhipāda* 471c13-14

Four *ṛddhipādas* 471c15-18

Base of power eştablished on stages of deliverance attained through concentration of Desire', what is Desire, what is concentration, what is deliverance, what is concentration of Desire, What is stage of deliverance, what is establishment through concentration of Desire'. 471c19-472c

As to 'Base of power established on stages of deliverance attained through concentration of Energy', what is 'Energy', what is 'concentration', what is 'deliverance', what is 'concentration of Energy', what is' deliverance', what is 'stage of deliverance', what is 'stage of deliverance', what is 'establishment through concentration of Energy 472c15-473c

As to 'Base of power established on stages of deliverance attained through concentration of Mind', what is 'mind', what is 'Concentration',what is 'concentration of Mind', What is 'deliverance', what is 'stage of deliverance', what is establishment through concentration of Energy'. 473c18-474c11

As to 'Base of Power established on stages of deliverance attained through Concentration of Investigation', what is 'Investigation', what is'concentration', what is 'Concentration of Investigation', what is 'deliverance', what is 'stage of deliverance', what is 'establishment through Concentration of Investigaton'. 474c12-475c6

Why those four are called'Base of Power' 475c7-23

Attainments of Bases of power.

Chapter-IX Bases of Mindfulness (*smṛtyupasthāna*)

Chinese Text

The Buddha's instruction on bases of *smṛtyupasthānas* 475c25-26

Four *smṛtyupasthāna* 475c26-476a

Kāyasmṛtyupasthāna 'when one dwells contemplating on body in the body' etc internally, Contemplating on body in the body externally, contemplating on body in the body etc.both internally and externally 476a4-c20

'*Vedanā-smṛtyupasthāna*',when a monk dwells contemplating on feeling in feeling etc.internally, contemplating on feeling in feeling etc. externally, contemplating on feeling in feeling etc. both internally and externally. 476c20-477 c 9

'*Citta-smṛtyupasthāna*', when a monk dwells contemplating on mind in mind etc. internally, contemplating on mind in mind etc. both externally and interally. 477 c 10 - 478 b 16

Dharma-smṛtyupasthāna', when a monk dwells contemplating on *dharma* in *dharma* etc. externally, contemplating on *dharma* in *dharma* etc. internally, contemplating on *dharma* in *dharma* etc.both externally and internally. 478b24-478b29

Chapter-X Noble truth (*āryasatya*)

The Buddha's instruction on *āryasatya* 479b25-26

Four *āryasatyas* 479b26-480a15

What is noble truth of 'suffering' 480a16-481a4

Birth, death,old age, object of attachment etc.

What is birth, death,old age, sickness etc.

What is noble truth of cause of suffering 481a5-29

Cravings

What is the Noble truth of Cessation 481b1-c6

Cessation of the cravings

What is the noble truth of the way for the 481c6-482a25

cessation of suffering

Eightfold path

Chapter-XI Meditative Absorption (*dhyāna*)

Chinese text

The Buddha's instruction on *dhyāna* 482a27-28

Four 'ways of heaven' for purification 482a29-b9

First 'way of heaven' when dwelling on theFirst *dhyāna* 482b10

Second 'way of heaven' when dwelling on the Second *dhyāna*

Third 'way of heaven' when dwelling on the Third *dhyāna*

Fourth 'way of heaven' when dwelling on the Fourth *dhyāna*

(First *dhyāna*)

what is 'detached from desire' 482b10

what is 'desire;

which are evil unwholesome *dharmas* 483a4-5

Five '*nīvaraṇas*' 483a5-b4

Accompanied by *vitarka* and *vicāra* 483b13-24

what is *vitarka*

what is *vicāra*

Detached from *sukha* and prīti' 483b24-c10

what is sukhā

what is *prīti*

what is 'first *dhyāna* 483c10-484a15

what is *dhyāna*

Sphere of First *dhyāna*

(*Second dhyāna*)

what is 'one subsiding *vitarka* and *vicāra'* 484a160-26

what is 'inner tranquility'

what is 'oneness of mind'

what is 'with out *vitarka* and *vicāra*'

what is 'concentration'

what is '*prīti* after the subsiding of *vitarka* and *vicāra'* 484a26-27

what is '*Sukha* after the subsiding of *vitarka* and *vicara* ' 484a27-28

What is *priti* and *sukha* born of concentration (*samādhi)* 484b1-3

what is 'second *dhyāna'* 484b3-4

sphere of second *dhyāna.* 484b5-17

(Third dhyāna)

'detached from *prīti*', 484b18-20

'dwells in *upekṣā* with *samyak smṛti* and *samyak jñāna*', 484b20-25

what is *upekṣā*

what is *samyak jñāna*

'one experiences bodily feeling of happiness' 484b26-29

'one accompained with *upekṣā* as said by the holy ones' 484b29-c3

'the holy ones'

'The third one' 484c3-4

'Dhyāna' *484c4-16*

Sphere of the Third *dhyāna.*

(Fourth dhyāna)

'one who abandones *sukha*' 484c17-19

What is *'sukha'*

'one who abandones *duḥkha'* 484c20-23

What is *duḥkha*

'Disappearance of previous *sukha* and *daurmanasya*' 484c23-29

what is *daurmanasya*

Attainment in entering the First *dhyāna* 484c29-485a5

Attainment in entering the Second *dhyāna*

Attainment in entering the Third *dhyāna*

Attainment in entering the Fourth *dhyāna*

'one purified by *upekṣā* and *smṛti'* 485a11-25

what is *upekṣā*

what is *smṛti*

what is 'purification'

'The fourth'

Chapter-XII The Immeasurable (*Apramāṇa*)

two kinds of '*karuṇā* concentration of mind' 486 c7 - 9

Development of 'Small *karuṇā* concentration of mind'
486c9-487a1

Development of 'Immeasurable *karuṇā* concentration of mind'
487a1

What is *muditā* 487a 23-28

Two kinds of '*muditā* concentration of mind' 487a29-b1

Development of 'Small *muditā* concentration of mind'
487b1-22

Development of 'Immeasurable *muditā* concentration of mind'
487b23-c14

What is *upekṣā* 487c15-18

What is the development of '*upekṣā* concentration of mind'
487c15-18

'Entering into *upekṣā* concentration of mind'

Two kinds of '*upekṣā* concentration of mind' 488 a1

Development of 'Small *upekṣā* concentration of mind'
488 a2-22

Development of 'Immeasurable *upekṣā* concentration of mind'
488 a2-b13

Chapter-XIII Formless Meditative Absorptions (*ārūpyāṇi*)

Chinese Text

The Buddha's instruction on *ārūpyas* 488b23-24

Four *ārūpyas* 488b25-c2

First *ārūpyas*, 'Sphere of Boundless Space'

Chapter - XIV Cultivations of Absorption (*bhāvanāsamādhi*)

What is *bhāvanāsamādhi* through which the monk attains excellent forms of *prajñā* 489 b 18 - 23

What is *bhāvanāsamādhi* through which the monk attains extinction of all the defilements 489 b 23 - c4

Analysis of the First *bhāvanāsamādhi* 489 c5 - 490 a 10

Analysis of the Second *bhāvanāsamādhi* 490 a11 - c23

Analysis of the Third *bhāvanāsamādhi* 490 c 24 - 491 a 20

Analysis of the Fourth *bhāvanāsamādhi* 491 a 21 - b 7

Chapter-XV Seven Factors of Enlightenment (*bodhyaṅga*)

Instructions of the Buddha on *bodhyaṅga* 491b9 - 12

What is *bodhyaṅga* 491b16 - 17

Seven *bodhyaṅgas* 491b18 - c2

Attainments of 7 factors. 491 c 3 - 17

'Mindfulness factor' as contemplating inside the body,

outside the body, both inside and outside the body.

'Mindfulness factor' as contemplating feeling.

Mindfulness factor as contemplating Mind.

Mindfulness factor as contemplating mind-object.

Attainments of Mindfulness factor

'Investigation of *Dharma* factor' as wisely investigating of the various *dharma*. 491 c 18 - 492 b 18

Wholesome *dharma*

Unwholesome *dharma*

Meritorious *dharma*

Demeritorious *dharma*

Dharma which is to be developed

Dharma which is not to be developed

Lowly *dharma*

Excellent *dharma*

Black *dharma*

'White' *dharma*

Dharma putting obstacles to mind

Dharma born of causes

Attainments of 'Investigation of *dharma*' factor.

'Energy Enlightenment Factor' 492b19-c 5

Arousing of mental energy when abandoning the evil unwholesome *dharmas.*

Arousing of mental energy when avoiding the arising of unwholesome dharmas that have arisen.

Arousing of mental energy when causing to appear the wholesome *dharmas* that have not arisen.

Arousing of energy to develop and maintain the wholesome *dharmas* which have arisen.

Attainments of 'Energy factor'

'Rapture Enlightenment factor' conditions for arising of supersensuous rapture leading to enlightenment 492 c 6 - 25

Attainments of Rapture enlightenment factor' in various stages of Buddhist Path. 492 c 26 - 493 b 27

'Tranquility enlightenment factor' 493c7-27

Tranquility arising in the first *dhyāna.*

Tranquility arising in the second *dhyāna.*

Tranquility arising in the third *dhyāna.*

Tranquility arising in the fourth *dhyāna.*

Tranquility arising in the fifth *dhyāna.*

Tranquility arising in the sixth *dhyāna.*

Developing 'Tranquility enlightenment factor'

as tranquility of body and tranquility of mind

'Concentration Enlightenment-factor' 493 c 27 - 494 b 14

Conditions for arising of 'concentration Enlightenment factor' in the first formless meditation - attainments. Conditions for arising of 'concentration Enlightenment factor' in the Second formless meditation - attainments. Conditions for arising of 'Concentration Enlightenment factor in the Third formless meditation - attainments

Conditions for arising of 'Concentration Enlightenment factor' in the Fourth formless meditation - attainments.

'Equanimity Enlightenment-factor' 494 b 15 - 29

Development of Equanimity

Enlightenment factor arising when being

completely detached from the worlds (*dhātu*)

and dwelling the contemplation of equanimity

Development of 'Equanimity Enlightenment-factor' arising when being completely detached from Attachment, Hatred, and Delusion, and dwelling the contemplation of equanimity.

Development of 'Equanimity Enlightenment factor' arising when the mind not receiving feeling regarding objects of Attachment,

Hatred and Delusion attainments of 'Equanimity Enlightenment factor'

Chapter XXVI Miscellaneous matters

Buddha's instruction on 78 defilements

	Chinese text
On *rāga*	494c20 - 22
On *dveṣa/pratigha/doṣa*	494c22 - 25
On *moha*	494c25 - 495a13
On *krodha*	495a14 - b2
On *upanāha*	495b2 - 6
On *mrakṣa*	495b6 - 15
On *pradāśa*	495b15 - 20
On *īrṣyā*	495b20 - 24
On *mātsarya*	495b25 - c6
On *māyā*	495c6 - 8
On *śāṭhya*	495c8 - 10
On *āhrīkya*	495c10 - 13
On *anapatrāpya*	495c13 - 15
On *māna*	495c15 - 17
On *atimāna*	495c17 - 19
On *mānātimāna*	495c19 - 20
On *asmimāna*	495c20 - 22
On *adhimāna*	495c22 - 24
On *ūnamāna*	495c24 - 25

On *mithyāmāna*	495c25 - 27
On *mada*	495c27 - 496a2
On *pramāda*	496a3 - 4
On *ao*	496a4 - 11
On *fen*	496a11 - 13
On *chiao wang*	496a14 - 17
On *lapana*	496a17 - b6
On *nemittakata* (Pali)	496b7 - 11
On *nispesikatā*	496b11 - 16
On *lābhena lābhah nijigisanata* (Pali)	496b16 - 21
On *pāpicchatā* (Pāli) *Vibh.* 416	496b21 - 26
On *mahicchatā* (Pāli)	496b27 - 28
On *atricchatā* (Pāli) *Vibh.* 416	496b28 - c5
On *pu - hsi - tsu*	496c5 - 7
On *pu - kung - ching*	496c7 - 15
On *daurvacasyatā*	496c15 - 24
On *pāpamitratā*	496c24 - 497a2
On *akṣānti*	497a2 - 6
On *tan - shih*	497a6 - 8
On *jan - tan*	497a9 - 10
On *adharmarāga*	497a10 - 12
On *cha-t'an*	497a12 - 13
On *pāparāga*	497a13 - 16
On *satkāyadṛṣṭi*	497a17 - 18

On *śāsvatadṛṣṭi*	497a18 - 19
On *ucchedadṛṣṭi*	497a20 - 21
On *kāmarāga*	497a21 - 24
On *vyāpāda*	497a24 - 25
On *styāna*	497a26 - 27
On *middha*	497a27 - 28
On *auddhatya*	497a28 - 29
On *kaukṛtya*	497a29 - b1
On *vicikitsā*	497b2 - 4
On *arati*	497b4 - 10
On *vijṛimbhikā*	497b10 - 11
On *bhakte 'samatā*	497b12 - 13
On *cetaso līnatva*	497b13 - 14
On *nānātvasamjñā*	497b14 - 17
On *ayoniśo manaskāra*	497b17 - 19
On *dausṭhulya*	497b19 - 22
On *ti - lu*	497b22 - c4
On *sringi*	497c5 - 6
On *tintilaka*	497c6 - 7
On *anarjavatā*	497c7 - 9
On *amārdavatā*	497c9 - 11
On *asabhāgānuvartana*	497c11-14
On *kāmavitarka*	497c15-17
On *vyāpādvitarka*	497c17-18

End of "the ninth *chüan* of the *Dharmaskandha -pādaśāstra* belonging to the *Sarvāstivāda* school."

Chapter - XVII On Controlling faculties (*indriya*)

Chapter - XIX On Aggregates (*skandha*)

Chapter - XX On Various Elements

On attaining knowledge of two elements (*sāsrava, anāsrava*) 502a5-6

On attaining knowledge of two elements (*samskṛta, asaṃskṛta*) 502a6-7

On attaining knowledge of twelve *āyatanas* 502a8-12

On attaining knowledge of five *skandhas* 502a12-15

On attaining knowledge of *pratītyasamutpāda* 502a15-27

On attaining knowledge of *āyatana* 502a 28-c15

On attaining knowledge of various elements 502c15-18

On *cakṣurdhādhātu, rūpadhatu,cakṣurvijñānadhātu* 502c18-22

On *pṛthvīrdhātu* 502c24-503a5

On *āpodhātu* 503a5-16

On *agnidhātu* 503a16 -29

On *Vāyudhātu* 503b12-20

On *Vijñānadhātu* 503b21-22

End of the "tenth chüan of the *Dharmaskandhapādaśāstra* belonging to the *Sarvāstivāda* school."

On *kāmadhātu* 503c5 - 10

On *vyāpādadhātu* 503c10 - 12

On *vihiṃsādhātu* 503c13-16

On *naiskramyadhātu* 503c17-504a10

On *avyāpādadhātu* 504a10-24

On *avihiṃsādhātu* 504a24-b8

On *sukhadhātu* 504b9-11

On *duḥkhadhātu* 504b12-13

Chapter - XXI On Dependent Origination

On *avidyā*-conditioned *puṇyasamskāra* among the *asaṃjñidevas* 506b26-c10

On *avidyā*-conditioned *āniṃjya saṃskāras* among the gods of the *ārūpya* heavens 506c11-26

On *saṃskāra* -condition of *vijñānas* 507a1-8

On *apuṇyasaṃskāra* as condition of *vijñāna* 507a9-13

On *puṇyasaṃskāras* as condition of *vijñānas* 507a14-29

On *apuṇyasaṃskāra*-conditioned *vijñānas* among being in different *kāma*-heavens and *rūpa*-heavens 507b1-6

On *puṇyasaṃskāra*-conditioned *vijñānas* in *ārūpya* heavens 507b6 - 21

On *nāmarūpa* conditioned through *vijñānas* 507b21 - c2

On reincarnative state of *nāmarūpa* conditioned through *vijñāna* 507c2-24

On *vijñāna* conditioned through *nāmarūpa* 507c25-29

On reincarnative state of *vijñāna* conditioned through *nāmarūpa* 508a1-b10

On *saḍāyatana* conditioned through *nāmarūpa* 508b11-23

On origination of *rūpa* or *mahābhūta* and *nāma* or *four skandhas* 508b23 - c2

On reincarnative state of *saḍāyatana* through *nāmarūpa* in realms of happiness for man etc. 508c17-20

On origination of *saḍāyatana* through *nāmarūpa* among the unconscious gods of *Brahmakāyika* etc. 508c22-28

On origination of *sadāyatana* through *nāmarūpa* among the unconscious gods of *Bṛhatphala* etc. 508c28-509a2

End of the "eleventh *chüan* of the *Dharmaskandha pādaśāstra* belonging to the *Sarvāstivāda* school."

On *sparśa* conditioned through *nāmarūpa*	509a9-15
On reincarnative state of *sparśa* conditioned through *nāmarūpa* associated with *ayoniśo manasikāra*	509a16-25
On origination of *sparśa* through *nāmarūpa* in hell etc.	509a26-b3
On origination of *sparśa* through *nāmarūpa* in the realms of happiness for man etc.	509b3-7
Origination of *sparśa* conditioned through *nāmarūpa* among the gods of *Brahmakāyika* etc.	509b9-14
On *adhivacanasāṃsparśa* and *pratighasāṃsparśa*	509b16-22
On *sparśa* conditioned through *saḍāyatana*	509b23-c2
On *sparśa* as "comiong together of the three"	509c3-10
On *vedanā* conditioned through *sparśa*	509c11-24
Three kinds of physical and mental *vedanā* conditioned through *sparśa*	509c25-510a12
On *tṛṣṇā* conditioned through physical and mental *vedanā*	510a13-29 511b1
On *upādāna* conditoned through *tṛṣṇā*	511b3
On *upādāna* conditoned through *kāmatṛṣṇā*	511b4-8
On *upādāna* conditioned through *rūpatṛṣṇā* and *arūpyatṛṣṇā*	511b8-12
The Buddha's teachings on discernment of *skandhas*	511b12-19
On *pratītyasamutpanna*	511b19-c3
On the development of attachment	
On *jāti* conditioned through *bhava* among the gods of the *Ārūpaya* heavens	513a9-17

The Buddha's dialogue with Ānanda on the purpose of *'jāti* conditioned through *bhava'*	513a18-26
On *jarāmaraṇa* conditioned through *jāti*	513a27-b14
On *śoka*	513b15-19
On *parideva*	513b20-26
On *duḥkha*	513b26
On *daurmanasya*	513b26-27
On *upāyāsa*	513b27-29
On arising of *duḥkha skandha*	513c1-10

End of the "twelth *chüan* of the *Dharma skandhapādaśāstra* belonging to the *Sarvāstivāda* school."

2. INSTRUCTIONS AND FAITH

A. Precepts (*śikṣāpadāni*)

Brodly speaking *śikṣāpadāni* (Chi. *hsueh-chu*) means "moral rules", The word *śikṣā* means 'training ' and the word *pāda* means 'steps'. Thus *śikṣāpada* means 'steps of training ' which refer to the five precepts or moral rules (also known as *pañcaśīla*) specially instructed for the Buddhist laymen and are included among the Ten precepts binding on the novices and monks.

Five Precepts :

The five precepts are :

Abstaining from killing

Abstaining from taking what is not given

Abstaining from engaging in unlawful sensuous lust

Abstaining from lying

Abstaining from taking intoxicants that causes indolence

Five precepts as preached by the Buddha

In its first chapter, the *ADSPS* mentions that the Buddha instructed five precepts while he was addressing the mohks during his stay in the Jeta grove at Anāthapiṇḍada's park in the city of Śrāvastī.

For the laymen, the purpose of the five precepts is to get rid of the five dreads (*bhaya, chinese hu*), enemies (*vaira*), or disturbances (*aśānta, pu-tsi-ching*) for which one is contemptible (*garhya, ko yen*) in this world. Not only this, even after death, he, with a different kind of body arises in hell to repent. The five dreads, taking life(*prāṇātipātaka, sha-sheng*) taking what is not given (*adattādāyika*), is given to sensuous lust (*kameṣumithyācāraka*), is given to lies (*mṛṣāvādaka*) taking intoxicants that causes indolence (*surāmaireyamadyapramādasthāyika).*

However, one who abstains from those five dreads, is praised as the virtuous in this world and after death arises among the gods in the heaven.

In a more detailed treatment on each of the five dreads, the *ADSPS* explains that the taker of life, conditioned by his taking life, breeds (*prasavati*) dread enmity. But he who abstains from taking life (*prānatipātāt prativiratasya*) , his first dread enmity is appeased. Likewise, one who takes what is not given to him, conditioned by his *adattādāna,* breeds dread enmity. But one who abstains from *adattādāna,* his second dread enmity is appeased. The rest three dreads are to be explained in the same way. In the *ADSPS* the *Dhammapada* in its Sanskrit version is also quoted in this context:

Yah prāṇam atipādayati mṛṣā vādam ca-bhāṣate loke adattaṃ ādatte paradāraṃ ca gacchati surāmaireyapānaṃ ca yo naro hy adhigṛdhyati śaktah pañcasu dharmeṣu duḥsile iti kathyate.

Lay Adherents

Upāsaka literally means 'sitting close by' (*Upa+ vas*) "who is filled with faith and has taken refuge in the Buddha, his doctrine, and his community of noble disciples." When he observes the five precepts he is considered as free of mental impurities.

The *ADSPS* explains that the layman with white clothes, a male, who after taking refuge in the Buddha, in the *dharma*, and in the *Saṅgha,* arouses his mind and pronouces these words,' consider me as an *Upāsaka'.* Only through this he becomes an *Upāsaka*(cf.454 a 15-17).

Upāsaka observing five rules

Five types of *upāsakas* are detailed in the *ADSPS* in terms of their observance of the rules:

Upāsaka of one rule (*ekadeśakārin*)

Upāsaka of two rules(*pradeśakārin*)

Upāsaka of three rules (*Yadbhūyaskārin*)

Upāsaka of four rules(*aparipūrṇakāri*)

Upāsaka of five rules (*paripurṇakārin*)

Thus the *upāsaka* who has taken refuge to the Buddha, the doctrine and the *Saṅgha* and is abstained from killing (one of the five precepts) but is not abstained from the four other precepts is the one who is engaged in observeing one rule (*ekadeśakārī*).

The *Upāsaka* who has taken refuge to the Buddha, the Doctrine and the Saṅgha, and is abstained from killing and abstained from taking what has been given to him(two of the five precepts) but is not abstained from the three other Precepts is the one who is known as *pradeśakārī* in the observance of the rules.

The *Upāsaka* who as taken refuge to the Buddha, the Doctrine, and the *Saṅgha,* and is abstained from killing, abstained from taking what has been given to him, and abstained from unlawful sensuous lust (i.e., three of the five precepts), but is not abstained from two other precepts is the one who is known as *yadbhūyaskārī* in the observance of the rules.

The *Upāsaka* who has taken refuge to the Buddha, the Doctrine and the *Saṅgha,* and is abstained from killing, abstained from taking what has not been given to him, abstained from engaging in unlawful sensuous lust, abstained from lying (i.e., four of the Precepts), but is not abstained from taking intoxicants that cause indolence, is known as *aparipūrṇakārī* in the observance of the rules.

The *Upāsaka* who has taken refuge to the Buddha, the Doctrine, and the *Saṅgha,* and is abstained from killing, abstained from taking what has not been given to him, abstain ed from engaging in unlawful sensuous lust, abstained from lying, abstained from taking intoxicants that cause indolence, is known as *paripūrṇakāri* in the observance of the rules.

Purpose of observance of Precepts by the *Upāsaka*

1. The *upāsakas* observing five Precepts establish (*samādāpayati*) only himself, not others, as he himself is abstained from the killing etc., but cannot make others to abstain from the same.

2. *Upāsaka* observing Ten Precepts accomplishes well-being for himself as well as of other , as he himself abstains from the Five dreads (killing etc), and also makes other to abstain from same.

3. *Upāsaka* observing fifteen accomplishes well-being for himself as well as others and also for the well-being of many

(*bahujanahitāya),* for the happiness of many (*bahujanasūkhāya*) as he himself abstains from the five dreads like taking life of others, makes others to abstain from the same and becomes very pleased (*sumanojña,*) to see the one who is abstained from taking life of others.

4. *Upāsaka* observing eight precepts accomplishes well-being for himself, not for others. He is endowed with faith (*śraddhā,*) but cannot establish others to be endowed with faith; he is endowed with moral observances (*śila*) and renuciation (*tyāga,*); he goes to nearly parks to visit the monks; he attentively listens to the doctrines; he retains the doctrines heard; he examines the meaning of the doctrines retained (in memory); he becomes convinced in the doctrines with other minor details for following the meaning of the doctrines and the doctrines. But he does not make others to observe the doctrines, or to be convinced in the doctrines with other minor details. Thus the *upāsaka* observing the eight rules accomplish his own well-being and not of others.

However, the *Upāsaka* observing sixteen moral rules and the *Upāsaka* observing twenty-four moral rules or Precepts accomplish well-being for both himself and others.

Destiny of Upāsaka

The *ADSPS* presents the details of the destinies of the *Upasaka* after death in terms of following the immoral things as against the observance of the moral rules.

The *Upāsaka* engaged in ten thing like the four dreads from taking life of others to lying, evil (*piśuna)* and rude (*paruṣa*) speech, engaged in (*Sambhinnapralāpa,* having wrong views (*mithyādṛṣṭika*) arises in hell because of difference of body after death.

The *Upāsaka* engaged in twenty immoral things like the ten (mentioned above) committing himself, and make others to commit those ten things, arise in hell because of difference of body after death.

The *Upāsaka* engaged in thirty immoral things like the twenty mentioned above added with ten more -being pleased with seeing the killing by himself and others (l), being pleased with seeing the committing of *adattādāna* up to being *mithyādrṣṭika* himself (9), arises in hell same destiny awaits.

the *Upāsaka* engaged with forty immoral thing like

(a) commits the ten things frcm taking life of others to having wrong views

(b) Makes others tc commit those ten immoral things

(c) Becomes pleased with those ten,

(d) Describes(*varnnam bhāṣate*) those ten.

On the other hand, the *Upāsaka* engaged in ten moral thing arises among the gods in the heaven after death as he abstains from taking life, from taking what is not given, from being engaged in unlawful sensuous lust, from lying, from speaking evil, from speaking rude, from *sambhinnapralāpa*, and attains *avyāpannacitta* etc., and right view.

The *Upāsaka* engaged in twenty moral things like the ten as mentioned above for himself and also making others to be engaged in the same also arises in the heaven.

The *Upāsaka* engaged in thirty moral things like the twenty mentioned above added with ten more-being pleased with seeing the non-killing by himself and others(1) and being pleased with seeing the abstination from *adattādāna* up to being *mithyādrṣtika* by himself (9) arises in heaven.

The *Upāsaka* engaged with forty moral things like

(a) Abstination from ten things, i.e., from *adattādāna* up to being *mithyādrṣṭika,*

(b) Makes others to abstain from the ten moral things,

(c) Becomes pleased to see the abstination from the ten.,

(d) Describes those ten arises in heaven.

B. Conditions to Stream-Entry (*srotāpattyaṅgāni, yü-liu-chih*)

The word *srota* means the river of stream and refers to the Buddhist path. It is the stream of *Nirvāṇa* as one goes by means of a stream. The ascetic who has entered into it, who has arrived at it, and who has attained it, is called "one who has entered into the stream (*srota-āpanna*). *Srotāpanna* is the lowest of the 8 noble disciples.

Early Buddhism recognises four stages of spiritual progress called *srotāpatti* (entering into the stream), *sakṛdāgāmī* (a stage of once-Returning), *anāgamī* (a stage of Non-Returning), and *arhant* (Holy life). These stages are the attainments of an adept as he overcomes one stage to another and obtains complete knowledge which is known as Arhathood.

An adept must possess specific qualities in order to become a *srotāpanna.* In the *Sotāpatti-saṃyutta* chapter of the *SN* (V,pp.262-64) it is said that one must have firm faith in the Buddha, *Dharma* and *Saṅgha* and must possess all the *śīlas,* liked and praised by the wise. These qualities are called *sotāpatti-aṅgas* (Skt. *srotāpattyaṅgas*). These qualities are to be possessed by a *sotāpanna* who has gone beyond the possibility of retrogression (*avimpatadhammo*) and destined to attain the highest knowledge (*niyato saṃbodhiparāyaṇo*).

The *sotāpatyaṅgas* are essential to the actual commencement of practices for attaining the stage of *srotāpatti.*

The *ADSPS* holds that entry into the stream (*srotāpatti*) needs four preliminary conditions which are called *srotāpatyaṅgāni,* rarely found in Pāli *nikāyas.*

1. The first condition is companionship with good persons

(*satpurusasaṃsevā*).

2. The second condition is hearing the good law (*Saddharmaśravaṇam*).

3. The third condition is wise reflection (*yoniśo manaskāra*).

4. The fourth condition is living in conformity with the law (*dharmānudhamapratipatti*).

C. *Attainments of Faith and Purity (avetyaprasāda, Cheng-ching)*

The word '*prasāda*' means 'faith' or 'purity' and '*avetya*' means to understand the qualities beforehand. So *avetyaprasāda* refers to firm faith/ purity-"A faith consecutive to the exact comprehension of the Truths."

The Stream-winner must attain four *avetyaprasādas* which are the acquisitions of faith and purity, these are -

1. The *avetyaprasāda* relating to the Buddha,
2. The *avetyaprasāda* relating to the *Dharma,*
3. The *avetyaprasāda* relating to the *Saṅgha*
4. The *avetyaprasāda* relating to the precepts dear to the saints.

'The *prasāda* relating to the Buddha' is a *prasāda* relating to the *aśaikṣa dharmas* which make up a Buddha.

'The *prasāda* relating to the *Saṅgha* is a *prasāda* relating to the *śaikṣa* and the *aśaikṣa dharmas* which make up the *Saṅgha.*

In the '*avetyaprasāda* relating to the *Dharma*', the *dharma* refers to the four noble truths. When one understands the noble truths, one attains the *avetyaprasāda* relating to *dharma.*

'The *prasāda* of morality' results from *prasāda* of the

mind.When the mind is thus convinced that one acquires the precepts.

The *avetyaprasāda* relating to the Buddha, the *Dharma*, and the *Saṅgha*, are faith(*śraddhā*) by their nature. The precepts dear to the *Aryāns*, are by nature morality (*sīla*). Thus they are two separate things. However both of the two is exclusively immaculate (*AK.* VI, 75).

D. *Fruits of the religious life (śrāmaṇyaphalāni, sha-men-kuo)*

Śrāmaṇya is the religious life, 'pure path' (*amala mārga*). By this path one becomes a *śramaṇa,* i.e., one who calms (*śamayati*) the defilements. The results of *śrāmaṇya* (*śrāmaṇyaphala*) are conditioned and unconditioned *dharmas. Phalas* are the moments which follows immediately as the result of the paths (i.e., *srotāpatti, sakṛdāgamī, anāgāmī,* and *arhant*). However, under certain conditons, those *phalas* may occur for number of times during life-time of a monk.

The fruitions are four in number :

1. Fruition of Stream-winning (*srotāpattiphala, yü-liu-kuo*)

2. Fruition of once-return (*sakṛdāgāmiphala, yi-lai-kuo*)

3. Fruition of Non-return (*Anāgāmīphala, pu-lai-kuo*)

4. Fruition of Holiness (*arhatvaphala, ā-lo-han-kuo*)

The results of *śrāmaṇya* are conditioned (*saṃskṛta*) and unconditioned (*asaṃskṛta),* As conditioned *dharmas,* the results are by nature *vimuktimarga* (path of Deliverance). As unconditioned *dharmas,* the result is *pratisaṃkhyānirodha.*

The conditoned results of *śrāmaṇya* are the eighty-nine *vimuktimārgas* which are 'outflowing result' *niṣyandaphala* of *śrāmaṇya.* There are eight paths of deliverance for the abandoning of the defilement to be abandoned through seeing (*darśanaheya, AK.* VI,27). Again, there are eighty-one paths of Deliverance, for the abandoning of the defilements abandoned through meditation (*bhāvanāheya*), i.e., the nine paths through which one abandons the nine categories of defilements of each of the nine spheres from *kāmadhātu* up to *bhavāgra.* These eighty-nine *vimuktimārgas* are the conditioned results of *śramaṇya.*

The *pratisaṃkhyānirodha* of the eighty-nine categories of defliements is the unconditoned result of *śrāmaṇya,* which is the virile result (*puruṣakāraphala. AK.*I I.56) of *śrāmaṇya.*

E. *Progress to Deliverance (abhijñāpratipad, tung-hsing)*

In the fifth section of the *ADSPS* four modes of progress in following the way to deliverance are detailed. The progress is determined in terms of *abhijñā* (comprehension). The four modes of progress are:

1. Painful progress with slow comprehension
2. Painful progress with quick comprehension
3. Pleasant progress with slow comprehension
4. Pleasant progress with quick comprehension

As it is explained in the *AN* IV .162-163, 166-169 etc:-

1. Some people by nature possess excessive greed, hate and delusion, and thus feels pain and sorrow. The five *indriyas,* i.e., faith (*śraddhā*) energy(*vīrya*) mindfulness (*smṛti*), concentration (*samādhi)* and wisdom (*prajñā*) are dull in him; thus he reaches slowly to the cessation of all passions.

2. Some people possess excessive greed, hate and delusion etc., but the five *indriyas* are sharp in him and so he reaches quickly to the cessation of passions.

3. Some people possess by nature no excessive greed etc., but the five mental faculties are dull in him, so he reaches slowly

to the cessation etc.

4. Some people possess by nature no excessive greed etc., but the five mental faculties are sharp in him, so he reaches quickly to the cessation etc.

(F) *Noble lineage (āryavamśa, sheng-chung)*

The word '*ārya*' means 'noble' and the word' *vamśa* means 'lineage'. In this way *āryavamśa* means 'noble lineage' and it refers to the classes of the Buddha's disciples. The *āryavamśas* are so called because the *Aryans* arise from them. They are non-attachment in their nature.

The four *Āryavaṃśas* are :

1. To be content with clothing (*cībarasantuṣṭisvabhāvaḥ*)
2. To be content with food (*piṇḍapātasantuṣṭisvabhāvaḥ*)
3. To be content with bed and with seat (*śayanāsanasantuṣṭisvabhāvaḥ*).
4. To take delight in Extinction /meditation (*prahāṇabhā-vanārāmatā*)

Among the four, the first three are contentment (*tuṣṭi*) by nature. The fourth one, however, is not contentment but is free from the attachment to pleasure (*kāmaraga*) and attachment to existence (*bhavāraga*).

With the teaching of the four *āryavamśas*, the Buddha established a certain mode of subsistence (*vṛtti*) and certain activities (*karma*) for his disciples who have left their old modes of subsistence and old activities to be engaged in the way to deliverance. He established the *vṛtti* in the first three *āryavamśas* and established *karma* in the fourth. He assured that if the activity was done with the *karma* established by him, the monks would obtain deliverance.

The purpose of establishing such *vṛtti* and *karma* was to create an obstacle to the arising of desire (*tṛṣnotpādavipakṣatah*). It has been established in the texts (*DN*. I I I, 228, *AN*. III. .16.248 etc.) that the arising of desire is fourfold: Desire arises by reason of clothing, of food, of the bed and seat, of existence and non-existence. The four *āryavamśas* were taught in order to create an obstacle to various desires.

The firsrt three *āryavamśas* for the time being arrest the desire for the things that one regards as pertaining to self (*mamakāra*). The fourth *āryavamśa* permanently arrests the desire of the object of the idea of self (*ahamkāravastu*) and of things pertaining to self.

3. PRACTICE AND ENLIGHTENMENT

A. *Right Striving (samyakpradhāna, cheng-ch'in)*

Samyakpradhāna is the right striving (*samyak =right, pradhāna = striving,* Skt. synonyms *utsāha, vīrya, prayatna* etc.) The four varieties of *samyakpradhānas* form the sixth stage of the *aṣṭangika mārga,* i.e. *samyakvyāyāma*). The path receives the name of *bodhipakṣika,*" containing the adjuncts of Bodhi" (enlightenment). There are thirty -seven *bodhipakṣikas* and the four *samyakpradhānas* are included in them.

The four *samyakpradhānas* are:-

1. The striving to avoid the unwholesome states that have arisen,
2. The striving to prevent the unwholesome states that may come in future,
3. The striving to develop the wholesome states that have arisen,
4. The striving to maintain or cultivate the wholesome states in future,

B. *Base of power (ṛddhipāda,sheng-tsu)*

The Sanskrit word *ṛddhi* (Pali, *iddhi*) means' power' or 'magical power' which refers to the supernormal knowledge obtained in the path. The four *ṛddhipādas* are the qualities or modes of obtaining the supernormal knowledge indicating the 'roads' to power.

According to the '*Sarvāstivādins, ṛddhi* designates absorption or *samādhi.* It is through *samādhi* that the modes of supernormal knowledge are attained.

The supernormal knowledge of *ṛddhi* is one of the three methods of conversion (*pratihārya*), i.e., "to carry off" (*har*), that is, to convert through miracles (*ṛddhipratihārya*).

The four *ṛddhipādas* are:

1. Concentration of Desire *(chandasamādhi, yü-san-mo-ti*),
2. Concentration of Energy (*vīrayasamādhi, tung-san-mo-ti*
3. Concentration of Investigation (*mīmāṃsāsamādhi, hsien(?) san-mo-ti*).

Chandasamādhi is so called because the monk, through making *chanda* (desire) a predominant factor (*adhipatipratyaya*) reaches concentration.

Vīryasamādhi is so called because the monk, through making *vīrya* (Energy) a predominant factor, reaches concentration.

Cittasamādhi is so called because the monk, through making *citta*(Mind) a predominant factor, reaches concentration.

Mīmāṃsāmādhi is so called because the monk, through making *mīmāṃsā* (Investigation) a predominant factor, reaches concentration.

Thus the four *ṛddhipādas* "indicate the road to power connected therewith. They form, by way of preparation, the roads to the power constituting the fruition of the path" (*Viś.* XI I).

It is said that the four *ṛddhipādas* "lead to the attaining and acquiring of magical power, to the power of magical transformation, to the generation of magical power, and to mastery and skill there in" (*Pts.*I I.205).

C. *Four bases of Mindfulness (smṛtyupasthāna, nien-chu-fa)*

The four bases of mindfulness are important aspects of cultivation of mind by a Buddhist monk when he develops supramundane absorption. *Smṛti* means 'Mindfulness' and *Upasthāna* refers to 'base', 'field', 'foundation'. There are four bases to which mindfulness is applied-*kāya* (body), *vedanā* feeling), *citta* (mind) and *dharma* (phenomena).

1. *Kāyasmṛtyupasthāna* is when a monk dwells (*chu*) contemplating on the impurities of the body by contemplating body in the body internally, externally, and both internally and externally. He is ardent (possessed with right Striving), aware (possessed of right View), and mindful (possessed of right Mindfulness). He has got rid of coveteousness and mental pain in the world.

2. *Vedanā-smṛtyupasthāna-vedanā* is feeling, arising from the contact between the sense-organs and the external objects. There are three kinds of feeling-*sukha, duḥkha*, and *aduḥkha-sukha. Vedanā-smṛtyupasthāna* is when a monk dwells contemplating on feeling in feeling etc. internally, and both internally externally. A monk learns to restrain and control all feelings, who practices Mindfulness with regard to feeling.

3. *Citta-smṛtyupasthāna*-dwells contemplating on *citta* (thought or mind) in *citta* etc. upto pain in the world internally

externally, both internally or externally. He perceives clearly any state of mind, whether it is greedy or not, hateful or deluded or not, constricted or scattered, surpassable or unsurpassable, concentrated or not concentrated, liberated or not liberated.

4. *Dharmasmṛtyupasthāna* is mindfulness with regard to the *dharmas* (mind-object, phenomena). A monk dwells contemplating on *dharma* in *dharma* etc. up to "pain in the world", internally, externally both internally and externally. He knows whether he has *kāma-chhanda,* how it is over come and how in future it does not arise. He knows whether he has *vyāpāda*, how it arises, how it is overcome, and how in future it does not arise. He knows whether he has *vicikitsā,* how it arises, how it is overcome, and how in future it does not arise. He knows whether one of the seven *bodhyaṅgas* is present in him or not, knows how it arises, and how it comes to full development. In this way the monk knows the *dharmas* which are obstacles to his mental vision and also knows how to over come them. He also knows the *dharmas* which are the factors of enlightment and how to develop them.

D. *Four Noble Truths*

The four Noble Truths are:-

1. The Noble Truth of suffering
2. The Noble Truth of cause of suffering
3. The Noble Truth of cessation of suffering
4. The Noble Truth of way leading to cessation of suffering

1. The Noble Truth of suffering is-Birth is suffering; ageing is suffering; sickness (physical and mental) is suffering; death is suffering, association with the disliked is suffering; separation from the liked is suffering; not to get what one seeks is suffering; in short, the five aggregates as the object of attachment are suffering (490a16-17)

What is birth? That which is this or that being in this or that category of sentient being is birth, genesis (*teng*), entry, appearance of the aggregates, acquiring of the elements, acquiring of the bases. This is called birth.

What is ageing? That which is being old, broken teeth, grey hair, wrinkled skin etc.

What is sickness or pain? That which is bodily pain, painful experience born of bodily contact, that which is mental uneasy, painful experience born of mental contact etc.

What is suffering of death? That which is this or that being in this or that category of sentient beings is death, passing away, the destruction of consciousness, completion of life span, the breaking up of the aggregates etc.

What is suffering that is association with the disliked? Whatever is disagreeable, unpleasant, etc. collaborating there with etc.

What is suffering that is separation from the liked? Whatever is agreeable, pleasent etc....not collaborating there with etc.

What is not to get what one seeks that is suffering? That which is not to get what is pleasent to senses and pleasant to mind.

2. The Noble Truth of cause of suffering is-that craving which is the cause of existence again, is accompained by lust and greed, is strong passion for this and that like craving for sense pleasure (*kāmatṛṣṇā*),craving for existence (*bhava-tṛṣṇā*), craving for non-existence (*vibhava-tṛṣṇā*).

3. The Noble Truth of cessation of suffering is the cessation of those cravings without residue.

4. The Noble Truth of way leading to cessation of suffering is the Noble path leading to cessation of suffering of the past,

future and present. This Noble path is eighfold Noble path : Right view, Right Thought, Right Speech, Right Action, Right Livelihood, Right Striving, Rightmindfulness, and Right Concentration.

Right View is knowledge of suffering, knowledge of cause of suffering, knowledge of cessation of suffering, knowledge of the way leading to the cessation of suffering.

Right Thought is investigation into *dharmas* (examination of things as they are).

Right Speech is abstaining from lying, abstaining from slanderous speech, abstaining from harsh words, and abstaining from foolish speech.

Right Action is abstaining from three physical evil. i.e.,abstaining from killing, abstaining from taking that which is not given, abstaining from sensuous lust.

Right Livelihood is a disciple making livelihood having abandoned wrong livelihood, abstaining from physical and vocal misconduct.

Right Striving is making effort, arousing energy, endeavour etc.

Right Mindfulness is a noble disciple is ardent, aware, mindful, not forgetting of the nature of *dharmas,* of the nature of remembering clearly etc.

Right concentration is mental absorption, not deluded, not distracted etc.

E. *Four Meditative Absorption (dhyāna, chen-hsu)*

Dhyana in general is defined as an application of a pure mind on a single object (*ekālambanatā, AKV,* 1126). In the *Sarvāstivāda* tradition, *dhyāna* is *prajñā or* wisdom . Because it is through *dhyāna* that an ascetic is 'concentrated' and 'He who is concentrated, knows truly.' *dhyāna* is means to know the nature of the *dharmas.*

In the eleventh chapter of the *ADSPS*, four "heavenly ways" (*tien-tao*) refer to the first four *dhyānas* which are absorptions of visible spheres (*rūpa-dhyāna*).

1. The first *dhyāna* is that when a monk detached from object of sensuous desire(*li-yü*), detched from objects of unwholesome state of mind(*li-pu-hai-fa*), enters into absorption, which is accompanied by *vitarka* and *vicāra,* and is born of detachment and filled with *prīti* and *sukha.*

2. After the subsiding of *vitarka* and *vicāra*, and by attaining inner (*nei*) tranquility and oneness of mind(*hsin-i-chu-hsing*), he enters into a state born of *samādhi* and free from *vitarka* and *vicāra;* and is filled with *prīti* and *sukha.*

3. After the detachment from *prīti,* he dwells in equanimity, with Right Mindfulness and clear consciousness; and he experiences in his body the feeling (as said by the Noble ones) of happiness of a man of equanimity.

4. After the abandonment of pleasure and pain, as the previous joy and grief disappears, the ascetic enters a state beyond pleasure and pain, the fourth absorptoin purified by equanimity and mindfulness.

F. Four Immeasurables (*apramāṇa, wu-liang*)

The *dhyānas* give rise to the four *apramāṇas.* The word *pramāṇa* means ' measure' and '*apramāṇa*' is that which is not measurable. In the Buddhist tradition, the four *apramāṇa* (Pāli, appamāna) designate the four boundless mental states-

1) Loving kindness (*maitrī*), 2) Compassion(*karuṇā,*)

3) Sympathetic Joy (*muditā,*), and4) Equanimity (*upekṣā,*).

These are also called four *Brahmavihāras.*

Loving kindness is described as follows - a monk with a mind full of loving kindness being free of hatred, enmity and harmfulnes with mind developed, unbounded, pervading first one direction, then a second, then a third and fourth, and thus above, below and every where.

The development of *karuṇā, muditā* and *upekṣā* are described in the same way. However, the natures of the four *apramāṇas* are different. *Maitrī* is mental freedom from malice (*alobha*), *karuṇā* is mental freedom from the same, *mudita* is mind accompained with joy that is satisfaction (*saumanasya*), and *upekṣā* is the absence of Desire (*alobha*).

G. Four Formless Meditative Absorption (ārūpya, wu-se).

Ārūpyas are " absence of physical matter" (*AKV* of VI I I.3). The meditation of *Ārūpypa* in their nature are application of pure minds on a single object". The four formless spheres are called Absorptions of the formless spheres. The four *ārūpyas* are-

1. Sphere of Boundless Space (*ākāśānāntya*)
2. Sphere of Boundless Conciousness (*vijñānānantya*)
3. Sphere of Nothingness (*ākimcanya*)
4. Neither-Notion-Non-Absence of Notion (*nāsaṃjñānāpyasaṃjñā*)

The first three are named so because in their preparatory exercises one considers space, consciousness and nothingness. In the fourth *ārūpya*, however, notions are very week; those are not active in it, neither it is completely without notions.

1. In the *ADSPS, the first ārūpya* is explained as follows, the monk, through the overcoming of the notions of form,

through the extinction of notion and no-attention to the notion of variety, he enters the sphere of Boundless Space and abides there.

2. Through the overcoming of the sphere of boundless space, the monk enters the sphere of boundless consciousness and abides there- the second *ārūpya.*

3. Through the overcoming of the sphere of boundless consciousness, he reaches sphere of Nothingness-The third *ārūpya.*

4. Through the overcoming of the sphere of nothingness he reaches the sphere of Neither-Notion-nor-Absence 0f notion-The fourth *ārūpya.*

H. Four Cultivations of the Absorption (*bhāvanāsamādhi, hsiu-ting*)

Bhāvanāsamādhi or *samadhibhāvanā* is " cultivation of the Absorption that culitvates, practices, repeatedly cultivates, which has for its result the possession of happiness in this world" (quoted in *AKV* of *AK* VI I I.27).

1. The 'first good *dhyāna* is the pure (*śuddhaka*) *dhyāna* through which the ascetic obtains " happiness in this world."

2. The second cultivation of the absorption has for its result the acquisition of the seeing of knowledge (*jñānadarśana*). This is the supernormal knowledge of the divine eye.

3. The third cultivation of the absorption has for its result the attainment of the excellent forms of *prajñā.* This is said to be *samādhibhāvanā* of superior qualities arising from cultivation,i.e., the qualities of the three spheres and pure qualities. The *samādhi* that produces these qualities is called *samādhibhāvanā.*

4. In the fourth absorption an absorption arises that is called the *vajropama samādhi* which destroyes all the defilements.

I. Seven Factors of Enlightenment (bodhyaṅgāni, chueh-chih)

The seven factors (*aṅga*) that lead to enlightenment(*bodhi*) are the following:

1. Mindfulness (*smṛti*) enlightenment-factor
2. Truth-investigation (*dharmavicaya*)
3. Energy (*vīrya*)
4. Rapture (*prīti*)
5. Tranquility (*praśrabdhi*)
6. Concentration (*samādhi*)
7. Equanimity (*upekṣā*)

1. Whenever the monk dwells contemplating inside the body, outside the body, and both inside and outside the body, mindful, clearly conscious after subduing greed and grief, his mindfulness is constant and undisturbed at such a time he has attained and is developing *smṛti-saṃbodhyaṅga.*

2. Whenever the monk, dwelling mindful investigates and examines the *dharmas* as whether those are wholesome or unwholesome, good or evil, to be developed or not to be developed etc.,......at such a time, he has attained and is developing *dharmavicaya-saṃbodhyaṅga.*

3. Whenever the monk, of his investigating thoroughly that some thing with wisdom, i.e., abandonment of evil and unwholesome *dharmas,* is firm and unshrinking....... at such a time he has attained and is developing *vīrya- saṃbodhyaṅga.*

4. Whenever in the monk, while firm in energy, arises supersensuous rapture, rejoicing, delight of consciousness etc..... at such a time, he has attained and is developing *prīti-saṃbodhyaṅga.*

5. Whenever of his enraptured mind, his body of mental

state becomes calm.....at such a time, he has attained and is developing *praśrabodhi-saṃbodhyaṅga.*

6. Whenever, being calm in mind, his mind becomes concentrated........ at such a time, he has attained and is developing *samādhi-saṃbodhyaṅga.*

7. Whenever, thus concentrated, he is well-balanced as he looks with complete indifference ...... at such a time he has attained and is developing *upekṣa-saṃbodhyaṅga.*

J. Defilements

In the Buddhist tradition it is said that suffering arises from various actions and these actions accumulate by reason of the *kleśas.* The *kleśas* also known as *anuśayas* (*proclivity*) which are the roots of existence. *Kleśas* are also known as *anuśaya.*

Kleśas continue in a series reproducing itself beginning with *rāga* (Attachment) and by reason of attachment the other *kleśa* place themselves in the series. The *kleśas* accomodate the spheres (*dhātu loka*) making the person fit for arising of the *kleśas.* Besides, the *kleśas* engender their' offsprings' which are called *upakleśas.* These *upakleśas* are defiled mental states included within the *saṃskāraskandhas.* In meditation onthe Extinction of suffering, an ascetic destroyes doubts on it which expels a certain category of *kleśas* and *upakleśas.* 78 types of these are enumerated in the sixteenth chapter entitled *Tsa-shih (kṣudraka-vastu)* of the *ADSPS,* which discusses the following mental faculties like *rāga, pratigha, vicikitsā, krodha, Upanāha, mrakṣa* etc. with various *saṃyojanas* like different types of *vitarka, paryeṣana* etc. The arrangement of the items are irregular. The mental faculties are discussed with definitions in the manner of some of those discussed in *Vibh.* Chapter 17, which is, however, more systematic in its exposition. The method of defining *kleśas* or the *saṃyojanas* in chapter 16 of the *ADSPS* shows *Sarvāstivādin* characteristics evident in the *Jñānaprasthānaśāstra.*

4. ESSENTIALS OF EARLY BUDDHIST PHILOSOPHY

The moral and mental disciplines cultivated as *śīlabhāvanā* and *samādhibhāvanā* by a Buddhist ascetic lead to the way of right understanding of the *dharmas* which is the cultivation of superior wisdom (*prajñābhāvanā*). During this cultivation, an ascetic attains the knowledge of theanalysis, classification, and the conditionality of all physical phenomena. The last five chapters (17-21) of the *ADSPS* considers the following subject matter of *prajñābhāvanā* which form the basis of the early Buddhist analytical philosophy-

1. Controlling Faculties (*Indriya, ken*)
2. Bases (*Āyatana, ch'u*)
3. Aggregates (*skandha, yün*)
4. Various Elements (*Nānādhātu, tuo-chieh*)
5. Dependent Origination (*pratītyasamutpāda, yün-ch'i*)

1. *Indriya*- The word *indriya* is derived from the root *idi* which signifies supreme authority. Whatever exercises supreme power or authority is called an *indriya.* Thus, in general, *indriya* signifies *adhipati* or ruler' (*AKV* intro. to *AK.* I I). In the *sūtras* and in the *Abhidharma* in Pāli and Sanskrit, *indriya* is a name for 22 partly physical partly mental phenomena. They are :

1. Controlling faculty of Eye (*cakṣurindriya*).
2. Controlling faculty of Ear (*śrotrendriya*).
3. Controlling faculty of Nose (*ghrāṇendriya*)
4. Controlling faculty of Tongue (*Jiḥvendriya*)
5. Controlling faculty of Body (*kāyendriya*)
6. Controlling faculty of Mind (*manendriya*)

7. Controlling faculty of Famininity (*strīrindriya*)
8. Controlling faculty of Masculinity (*puruṣendriya*)
9. Controlling faculty of Vitality (*Jīvitendriya*)
10. Controlling faculty of Bodily Pleasure (*sukhendriya*)
11. Controlling faculty of Bodily pain (*duhkḥendriya*)
12. Controlling faculty of Mental Pleasure (*saumanasyendriya*)
13. Controlling faculty of Mental pain (*daurmanasyendriya*)
14. Controlling faculty of Indifference (*Upekṣendriya*)
15. Controlling faculty of Confidence (*śraddhendriya*)
16. Controlling faculty of Energy (*vīryendriya*)
17. Controlling faculty of Mindfullness (*smṛtīndriya*)
18. Controlling faculty of Concentration (*samādhīndriya*)
19. Controlling faculty of Wisdom (*jñānendriya*)
20. Controlling faculty of the assurance: 'I shall know what I did not yet know' (*anajñātamājñ āsyāmīndriya*)
21. Controlling faculty of highest knowledge (*ajñendriya*)
22. Controlling faculty of final enlightenment (*ajñātāvīndriya*)

1-5 and 7-8 are physical ; No.9 is either physical or mental, all the rest are mental.

The *ADSPS* follows the methods of the *Vibh.,* as it asked, " what is *cakṣurindriya?*The answer is given on that, with regard to *rūpa*, that which was, is and will be seeing..... and so on.

The rest of the *indriyas* are dealt in the same way.

2. *Āyatna- Āyatana* is a name for the 12 bases or sources on which depend the mental process. There are six personal (*ādhyā-tmika*) bases which consist of five physical sense-organs and consciousness. The six outer (*bāhyārtha*) bases are the six objects. The 12 bases are:

Eye, or visual organ	visible object
Ear, or auditory organ	sound
Nose, or olfactory organ	odour
Tongue, or gustatory organ	taste
Body, or tactile organ	body-impression
Mind-base, or consciousness	Mind-object

Like the *indriyas*, the *āyatanas* are also explained in details with question and answer (cf. Vibh.II).

3. *Skandha- Skandha* is the name for the 5 Aggregates (groups of existence) with which all the mental and physical phenomena are summed up by the Buddha. These 5 *skandhas* appear to be an ego to the ignorant man:-

1. Material Existence Aggregate (*rūpaskandha*)
2. Feeling Aggregate (*vedanāskandha*)
3. Notion Aggregate(*saṃjñāskandha*)
4. Mental Impression Aggregate (*saṃskāraskandha*)
5. Consciousness Aggregate (*vijñānaskandha*)

1. *Rūpaskandha*-whether that has *rūpa* or form, is composition of four *mahābhūtas* (Great Matter)i.e., water, air, fire, and earth. That which is composed of the four *mahābhūtas*, is called *Rūpaskandha(se-yün).*

2. *Vedanāskandha- Vedanā* is that which is feeling, similar

to feeling, every other feeling, of the nature of feeling, feeling which is accepted. This is called *vedanāskandha*(*shou-yün*).

The various possible aspects of feeling are included in the *vedanāskandha.* These are as follows:

Two fold Division -

Kāyiki (bodily) *vedanā, shen-shou*

Caitasiki (mental) *vedanā, hsin-shou*

Three fold Division-

śātā (agreeable) *vedanā, yu-wei-shou*

Aśātā (neutral) *vedana, she-shou*

Sukhā (pleasant) *vedanā, le-shou*

Duḥkhā (painful) *vedanā, ku-shou*

Aduḥkhasukhā (neither painful nor pleasant) *vedanā pu-ke-pu-le-shou*

Four fold Division-

Kāmadhātuvedanā, yü-chieh- shou

Rūpadhātuvedanā, se-chieh-shou

Arūpyadhātuvedanā, wu-se-chieh-shou

Five fold Division-

Sukhendriya(faculty for feeling pleasure) *le-shou*

Duḥkhendriya (faculty for feeling pain) *ku-shou*

Saumanasyendriya (faculty for feeling satisfaction) *hsi-sho*

Daurmanasyendriya (faculty for feeling dissatisfaction)

yu-shou

Upekṣendriya (faculty for feeling no-unpleasure no-pleasure) *she-shou*

Six fold Division-

Cakṣusaṃsparśajā vedanā
Srotrasaṃsparśajā vedanā

Ghṛaṇasaṃsparśajā vedana

Jiḥvāsaṃsparśajā vedanā

Kāyasaṃsparśajā vedanā
Manasaṃsparśajā vedanā

3. *Saṃjñāskandha -Samjñā* is that which is notion, similar to notion etc. That is called *saṃjñāskandha* (*hsing-yün*). Through the direct contact of six sense organs, six kinds of notion are possible. They are:

1. *Cakṣusaṃsparśajā saṃjñā*
2. *Śrotrasaṃsparśajā saṃjñā*
3. *Ghrāṇasaṃsparśajā saṃjñā*
4. *Jihvāsaṃsparśajā saṃjñā*
5. *Kāyasaṃsparśajā saṃjñā*
6. *Manaḥsaṃsparśajā saṃjñā*

4. *Vijñānaskandha—Vijñāna* is that which is consciousness, similar to etc. That is called *vijñānaskandha.* The various possible aspects of *vijñāna* are included in the *Vijñānaskandha* (*shih-yün*) which comprises six classes of *vijñāna.* They are :

1. *Cakṣurvijñāna*
2. *Śrotravijñāna*

3. *Ghrāṇavijñāna*

4. *Jiḥvāvijñāna*

5. *Kāyavijñāna*

6. *Manovijñāna*

5. *Saṃskāraskandha*—In general six classes of volitions (*cetanā*) are called *saṃskāras* or *saṃskāraskandha*, (*hsing-yün*, *AKV.*, p. 37). The *ADSPS* explains two types of *samskāraskandha*, i.e.

1. *Cittasaṃprayuktasaṃskāra* (*hsin-hsiang-ying-hsing-yün*)

2. *Cittaprayuktasaṃskāra* (*hsin-pu-hsiang-ying-hsing-yün*)

1. The *dharmas* as *cetanā*, *sparśa*, *manaskāra* upto *mati* etc. and other similar *dharmas* associated with *citta* are called *citta-saṃprayuktasaṃskāraskandha* (For details, Chap. I of the *ADSPS*)

2. The *dharmas* as *prāpti*, *āsaṃjñi samāpatti* and others upto *nāmakāya* and other similar *dharmas* (i.e., *aprāpti*, *sabhāgata*, *āsaṃjñika*, *nirodhasamāpatti*, *jīvita*, *jāti*, *sthiti*, *jarā*, *anityatā*, *padakāya* and *vyañjanākāya*), which are not associated with *citta* are called *citta viprayukta saṃskāraskandha*.

4. *Various Elements*—The twentieth chapter of the *ADSPS* explains sixty-two Elements or *dhātus*. The Buddha gave the triple analysis of the *dharmas* in the way of *skandha*, *āyatana* and *dhātu* for a clear understanding of the nature and function of the *dharmas*. For the *Vaibhāṣikas* "*Dhātu* is that which carries, *dadhāti*", (*Vibhāṣā*, I. 27, p. 387b26-27) a *svalakṣaṇa* (own-characteristics). Principal *dhātus* are 18 in number. The *Bahudhātuka* (*Madhyamāgama*, T, p. 723c13) and the *ADSPS* enumerate 62 *dhātus* which were arranged within the 18 *dhātus* later in the *AK*.

The 18 *dhātus* (principal *dhātu*)—

1. *Cakṣurdhātu* (*yen-chieh*)
2. *Rūpadhātu* (*se-chieh*)
3. *Cakṣurvijñānadhātu* (*yen-shih-chieh*)
4. *Śrotradhātu* (*erh-chieh*).
5. *Śabdadhātu* (*sheng-chieh*)
6. *śrotravijñānadhātu* (*erh-shih-chieh*)
7. *Ghrāṇadhātu* (*pi-chieh*).
8. *Gandha* (*hsiang-chieh*)
9. *Ghrāṇavijñānadhātu* (*pi-shih-chieh*)
10. *Jiḥvādhātu* (*she-chieh*)
11. *Rasadhātu* (*wei-chieh*)
12. *Jiḥvāvijñānadhātu* (*she-shih-chieh*)
13. *Kāyadhātu* (*shen-chieh*)
14. *Spraṣṭavyadhātu* (*ch'u-chieh*)
15. *Kāyavijñānadhātu* (*shen-shih-chieh*).
16. *Manodhātu* (*i-chieh*)
17. *Dharmadhātu* (*fa-chieh*)
18. *Manovijñānadhātu* (*i-shih-chieh*)

Six Elements

19. *Pṛthvīdhātu (ti-chieh)*
20. *Āpodhātu (shui-chieh)*
21. *Tejodhātu (huo-chieh)*
22. *Vāyudhātu (feng-chieh)*

23. *Ākaśadhātu (kung-chieh)*

24. *Vijñānadhātu (shih-chieh)*

Six Elements

25. *Kāmadhātu (yu-chieh)*

26. *Vyāpādadhātu (hui-chieh)*

27. *Vihiṃsādhātu (hai-chieh)*

28. *Naiṣkramyadhātu (wu-yü-chieh)*

29. *Avyāpādadhātu (wu-hui-chieh)*

30. *Avihiṃsādhātu (wu-hai-chieh)*

Six Elements

31. *Sukhadhātu*

32. *Duḥkhadhātu*

33. *Saurmanasyadhātu*

34. *Daurmanasyadhātu*

35. *Upekṣādhātu*

36. *Avidyādhātu*

Four Elements

37. *Vedanādhātu*

38. *Saṃjñādhātu*

39. *Saṃskāradhātu*

40. *Vijñānadhātu*

Three Elements

41. *Kāmadhātu*

42. *Rūpadhātu*

43. *Arūpyadhātu*

Three Elements

44. *Rūpadhātu*

45. *Ārūpyadhātu*

46. *Nirodhadhātu*

Three Elements

47. *Atītadhātu*

48. *Anāgatadhātu*

49. *Pratyutpannadhātu*

Three Elements

50. *Hīnadhātu*

51. *Madhyamadhātu*

52. *Praṇītadhātu*

Three Elements

53. *Kuśaladhātu*

54. *Akuśaladhātu*

55. *Avyākṛtadhātu*

Two Elements

56. *Śaikṣadhātu*

57. *Aśaikṣadhātu*

58. *Naivaśaikṣa-nāśaikṣaidhātu*

Two Elements

59. *Sāsravadhātu*

60. *Anāsravadhātu*

Two Elements

61. *Saṃskṛtadhātu.*

62. *Asaṃskṛtadhātu*

5. *Pratītyasamutpāda-* The Sanskrit word *Pratītyasamutpāda* literally means " production by dependence", The Chinese synonym of *Pratītyasamutpāda* is *yüan-ch'i* which means" arising through conditons". Thus *pratītyasamutpāda* is the doctrine of conditionality of all mental and physical existences. This is a law of causation which provides insight into the Buddhist teaching of *anātmā* (not-self) and *anitya* (Impermanence).

In the beginning of the twenty first chapter of the *ADSPS* on *pratītyasamutpāda*, the Buddha explains *pratītyasamutpāda* in two ways -1. If that exists, then this exists *(i-tse-yu-p'i-yu)* and 2. From the arising of that, this arises(*tse-sheng-ku-p'i-sheng*). The first explanation is approved by Vasubandhu (*AKV,* p.457) while the second explanation is given by the *Sautrāntikas* (Poussin, *AK*,I I I , Foot note 206).

The *ADSPS* describes *Pratītyasamutpāda* in the following way:- *Avidyāpratyayā saṃskārāḥ (wu-ming-yüan-hsing)-"* through ignorance are conditioned the *saṃskārās* i.e., volitions that produced rebirth' *Saṃskārapratyayaṇ vijñānam (hsing-yüan-shih)-"* through the volitions is conditoned consciousness. "

Vijñānapratyayaṃ nāmarūpaṃ (shih-yüan-shing-se) - 'through the consciousness is conditioned mental and physical existences." (*nāma-rūpa*)

Nāmrūpapratyayam sadāyatanam (ming-se-yüan-liu-ch'u) - "

through the mental and physical existences are conditioned the six bases", i.e. five physical sense-organs and the sixth is consciousness.

Sadāyatanapratyayaḥ Sparśaḥ (liu-ch'u-yüan-ch'u) - " through the six bases is conditioned the contact or Impression."

Sparśapratyayā vedanā (ch'u-yün-shou) -" thro̶ugh contact is conditoned feeling.

Vedanāpratyayā tṛṣṇā (shou-yüan-yu) -" through feeling is conditioned craving."

Tṛṣṇā pratyayādupādānaṃ (chu-yüan-yu) -" through craving is conditioned clinging."

Upādānapratyayād jāti (yu-yüan-sheng) - " through clinging is conditioned the birth."

Jāti pratyayā jarāmaraṇam (sheng-yüan-lao-tse) -" through birth is conditioned old age and death."

Finally *Fa-sheng-t'i-t'an-k'u-yu-lao-nao,* through (old age and death) developing birth of trouble, lamentation, sorrow, grief, disturbance and vexation.

This scheme of *pratītyasamutpāda* is detailed in the *ADSPS* as follows:

1. Through *avidyā* is conditioned the *saṃskāras,* i.e.,

a) The state of *lobha,* the state of *dveṣa*, and the state of moha as *avidyā* is the cause of *lobha, dveṣa* and *moha.*

b) The wholesome *(kuśala)* unwholesome *(akuśala)* actions of body, speech and mind

c) The meritorious actions (i.e., the bodily and verbal actions, mind-state and mental states, *cittaviprayuktasaṃskāras* etc. which are wholesome); the demeritorious actions(i.e., the bodily and verbal actions, mind-state and mental states, *cittaviprayuktasaṃskāras,* which are unwholesome); neutral (*āniñjya*) actios (i.e., the meditations on the four immaterials,*ārupya*).

2." Through *saṃskāras* is conditioned consciousness", means that the *saṃskāras* are the causes of future rebirth in a suitable sphere (*gati*). The *ADSPS* explanation is as follows:

a) Depending on *saṃskāras* co-arising with all kinds of *lobha,* the consciousness co-arising with *lobha* is produced. In the same way, depending......*dveṣa*.......*dveṣa* is produced; depending......*moha*....*moha* is produced;

b) Depending on *saṃskāras* co-arising with all kinds of *alobha*......*adveṣa*....... *amoha*........ the consciousness....... *alobha*......*adveṣa*......*amoha*...... is produced

c) The meritorious and demeritorious, *saṃskāras* or actions produce their resultant (*vipākaja*) consciousness as eye-consciousness(seeing) etc upto mind-consciousness. Depending on the karmically neutral *saṃskāras* are conditioned the consciousness in the sphere of the Immaterials.

3) *Vijñānapratyayaṃ nāmarūpam* - '*nāma*' means mental phenomena resulting from *saṃskāras* or action, like *vedanā, saṃjñā, cetanā, sparśa, manaskāra.* The word signifies four *mahābhūtas* and the '*rūpa*' dependant thereon. Thus without consciousness there can be no physical and mental existence. Mental phenomena is always conditioned through consciousness. However, *rūpa* is conditioned through conciousness only at the moment of conception. Thus *nāmarūpa* is made up of five *skandhas* in the womb, from arising (at the moment of reincarnation), as long as the four organs (eye etc.) are not manifested. Two other organs, *manāyatana* and *kāyāyatana* exist from conception.

The *ADSPS* states that it is the ultimate *citta* of a *gandharva* which confusingly attributes (*sammūrchayati* ?) 'I-ness' (*ātmabhava*) immediately to *kalala* in mother's womb and confuses *kalala* as own *rūpa* and *Nāma* (the rest four aggregates). This *nāmarūpa* co-arising with *ayoniśa manaskāra*, thus conditioned by consciousness, arises in mother's womb. If there is no consciousness as the base of *nāmarūpa*, then there would be no arising of *bhava, jāti* etc.

4) *Nāmarūpapratyayaṃ saḍāyatanaṃ*—'*Āyatana*' refers to base or the sense-organs. Six *āyatanas* are six sense-organs *cakṣu, śrotra, ghrāṇa, jiḥvā, kāya* and *mana.* According to the *ADSPS*, *Nāmarūpapratyayaṃ saḍāyatanaṃ* is the state when the six senses are formed in the mother's womb. The formation of *saḍayatana* is detailed in various ways in the *ADSPS* as :

When the embroy gets heated from coldness, then the four great elements co-arise with heat conditioned by *nāmarūpa* (*rūpa* being the four *mahābhūtas* and *nāma* being the four aggregates born of the *mahābhutas*) which coarises with coldness, there is growth of the six organs. This is "*saḍāyatana* conditioned by *nāmarūpa*".

Karmically unwholesome *nāmarūpa* produces suffering of body and mind in future existence while karmically wholesome *nāmarūpa* produces pleasures of body and mind in future existence. This is *saḍāyatana* conditioned by *nāmarūpa.*

5) *saḍāyatanapratyaya sparśa*—Through the *saḍāyatana* is conditioned the physical and mental contact. This is the state when the six organs come in contact with their respective objects Contact is *sannipāta* of three - sense-organ, its object and *vijñāna.*

6) *Sparśapratyayā vedanā*—Through six *sparśas* are conditioned six feelings — five physical and one mental. Contact for feeling of pleasure conditons the feeling of pleasure (*sukhā vedanā*); contact for the feeling of pain conditions the feeling of pain (*duḥkhā vedanā*); contact for the feeling of no-pleasure no-pain conditions the feeling of no-pleasure no-pain.

7) *Vedanāpratyayā tṛṣṇā*—Through *Vedanā* is conditoned

the state of craving. Craving is attachment to objects, both physical and mental conditioned feeling, (whether agreeable, disagreeable, or neutral) repeatedly being favourable to the object and repeatedly being favourable, arises attachment to it. This is *vedanāpratyayā tṛṣṇā. Tṛṣṇā* is of two types—*bhavatṛṣṇā and vedanāpratyayātṛṣṇā.*

8) *Tṛṣṇāpratyayaṃ upādānaṃ* or clinging is intensified form of *tṛṣṇā.* It is of four kinds—1) clinging to sensuous lust (*kāmatṛṣṇā*), 2) clinging to erroneous views, 3) clinging to rules and rituals, and 4) clinging to personality—belief. Again through craving for heavenly rebirth etc people may be induced to cling to certain rules and rituals to reach the object of their desires.

9) *Upādanapratyayā bhava*—Through clinging or under the influence of strong desire one collects good or evil actions capable of producing future existence (*bhava*). This is twofold-originating existence (*utpattibhava*) and *karma* existence (*karmabhava*).

10) *Bhavapratyayā jātiḥ*—Through *bhava* is conditioned reincarnation, i.e., to enter into mother's womb again, and to appear in the world to experience meritorious and demeritorious actions.

11) *Jātipratyayā jarāmaraṇa* etc—Reincarnation conditions *jarā* (old age), the state of the *karma*—formation being old; conditons *maraṇa*, death, breaking up of existence ; conditioning grief over death of near and dear ones; conditioning lamentation over deaths of relatives like mother, father etc; condition of grief that is feeling associated with the five consciousnesses; condition of disatisfaction (*daurmanasya*) that is feeling associatied with *manovijñāna.*

The law of *pratītyasmutpāda* explains the " arising of the whole mass of suffering" (*duḥkhaskandha*) as follows.

Because of the mass of sufferingof *avidyā* , the mass of

sufferingof *saṃskāras* arises;

Because of the mass of suffering of *saṃskāra,* the mass of suffering of *vijñāna* arises;

Because of the mass of suffering of *vijñāna*, the mass of suffering of *nāmarūpa* arises;

Because of the mass of suffering of *nāmarūpa*, the mass of suffering of*sadāyatana* arises;

Becauseof the mass of sufferingof *sadāyatana*, the mass of suffering of *sparśa* arises;

Because of the mass ofsuffering of *sparśa,* the mass of suffering of *vedanā* arises;

Because of the mass of suffering of *vedanā,* the mass of suffering of *tṛṣṇā* arises;

Because of the mass of suffering of *tṛṣṇā*, the mass of suffering of *upādāna* arises;

Because of the mass of suffering of *upādāna*, the mass of suffering of *bhava* arises;

Because of the mass of suffering of *bhava*, the mass of suffering of*Jāti arises;*

Because of the mass of suffering of *Jāti*, the mass of suffering of *jarāmaraṇa* arises.

5. THE CHINESE *ADSPS* AND ITS PARALLEL TEXTS IN PĀLI AND SANSKRIT WITH SOME COMPARATIVE NOTES ON THE ADSPS

The *ADSPS* is one of the early*Sarvāstivāda Abhidharma*

text as is evident from its treatment on various *Ābhidharmic* topics, contents, structure and method of *Ābhidharmic* definition and elaboration. The basic *Ābhidharmic* tendencies of the text are clearly traceable in its contemporary and later *Abhidharma* texts. However, a careful study of the text also helps one to identify some salient features of the text itself.In the same way, inspite of some striking similarites with the Pāli *sutta* and the *Abhidhamma* texts, the *ADSPS* retains its sectarian character derived from the *āgamas* and culminating in the *Abhidharmakośa*, the great work by Vasubandhu, with his auto-commentary along with *Sphutārthā* commentary on the *AK* by Yaśomitra.

The ADSPS and the Sutta/ Sūtra literature

From the analysis of the contents and the exposition of the doctrines of the *ADSPS*, we may observe that the *ADSPS*, although considered as the text ofthe *śāstra*(commentarial literature) tradition, is very close to the *suttas* or the *sūtras* which are analytical in forms and contents. Poussin (introduction,*AKB)* holds that the *ADSPS* is a collection of the *sūtras.* The *ADSPS* in general takes topics from the *sūtras*, particularly preached by the Buddha in the Jeta Grove at Anāthapiṇḍada's Park. The topics are then reclassified and defined with greater details. For the elaboration of subject matter, quotations are taken from other texts. Out of 21 chapters of the *ADSPS,* 19 chapters are virtually other editions of the *sūtras/suttas* of the *Āgamas* and the *Nikāyas.* The sixteenth chapter entitled '*Tsa-shih*', classifies 78 types of defilements which is not found in a *sūtra* form. However, it is probable that the *ADSPS* collected and classified the various types of defilements described in the different texts of the Buddhist Canon. As far as the seventeeth chapter of the *ADSPS* on the *indriyas* is concerned, generally the *suttas* (for example, *SN.* XL VIII) explain only 19 *indriyas*, whereas the *ADSPS* collectes the references on other three *indriyas* and classifies twenty-two *indriyas* with details on them.

As mentioned earlier (p.17), any topics in the Chinese version of the *Chachakkasutta* (*MN* III, 280-87) correspond to the chapters in the *ADSPS* (details in Watanabe, pp. 54-55)

Comparison with Vibhaṅga

The *Vibhaṅga* is one of the early *Abhidhamma* text of the *Theravādins.* The work consists of 18 treatises (*vibhaṅga*). It explains the important items of Buddhist doctrine which are also treated in the *ADSPS.* These are :-

The five *skandha*

The twelve *āyatana*

The eighteen *dhātu*

The four *sacca*

The twenty-two *indriya*

The twelve *paṭiccasamuppāda*

The seven *bojjhaṅga*

The four *sammappadhāna*

The four *iddhipāda*

The *ariya aṣṭāṅgika magga*

The *jhāna,* the *appamaññna* etc.

However, in the exposition of the doctrines the *ADSPS* follows the method of quoting and explaining the texts of the *Āgamas* (*Sarvāstivāda* counterpart of the Pāli *suttas*). On the other hand, the *Vibhaṅga* uses three types of explanation -1) *sutta* explanation (*suttanta -bhājanīya*), 2) *Ābhidhammic* explanation (*abhidhamma-bhājanīya*), 3) *Pañhapuccha* explanation through 122 *mātikas* in the form of question and answer. Thus each *vibhaṅga* has three parts mentioned above.

Inspite of the fact that both the texts have striking

similarities, regarding the treatment of the subject-matter and manner of *ābhidhrmic* definition and elaboration besides the arrangement of topics, they show differences.

The main topic of the *ADSPS* is the moral and practical *dharmas* which are elaborated in the first fifteen chapters of the *ADSPS.* Specially the first three chapters discuss the teachings on practices and attainments of the laymen and novices, among which only the five precepts are included in the fourteenth chapter of the *Vibh.* The fourth, the fifth, and the fourteenth chapters of the *ADSPS,* i.e., *abhijñāpratipada, āryavaṃśa,* and *bhāvanā,* related mainly to practical aspects of the Buddhist training, are not seen in the *Vibh.* On the other hand, the first six chapters of the *Vibh.,* i,.e., *kandha, āyatana, dhātu, sacca, indriya* and *paccayākāra* coherently present the Buddhist epistemology, world- view, and psychology. The *ADSPS* discusses those topics in nineteenth, eighteenth, twentieth, tenth, and seventeenth chapters respectively, thus offering some what loose kind exposition of the theoretical *dharmas.* The chapters 7-15 of the *ADSPS* centers around the 37 *bodhipaksīya dharmas* and other paths of practice which are included in the chapters 7-11 of the *Vibh.*

In the *Vibh.*, the three types of discipline, i.e., *śīla, samādhi* and *prajñā* are dealt in the twelfth, thirteenth, fourteenth, fifteenth and the sixteenth chapter corresponding to the eleventh, twelfth, first etc., as the fifteenth and sixteenth are absent in the *ADSPS* . The sixteenth chapter in the *ADSPS* , i.e., *tsa-shih,* contains the *kleśas* which are also defined in the *khuddakavatthu,* the seventeenth chapter of the *Vibh.*

The AK and the ADSPS

The *Abhidharmakośa* by Vasubandhu with his auto-commentary along with *Sphutārthā* commentary on the *AK* by *Yaśomitra* is the most systematic set of work of later *Sarvāstivāda Abhidharma.* The *AK* explains the early *Ābhidharmic* doctrines in a detailed manner in its nine *kośasthānas.* Moreover it contains criticisms of the doctrines advocated by other school of Buddhist and non-Buddhist philosophy on various issues. This is a significant departure from the early seven *Abhidharmic* texts including the *ADSPS.*

The structure of the *AK* is different from that of the *ADSPS.* The *AK* has nine chapters, eight chapters consisting of about 600 *kārikās*, while the ninth chapter is composed in prose. The nine chapters are-

1. *Dhātunirdeśa* (a treatment of elements of mental and physical things.)

2. *Indriyanirdeśa* (a treatment of the controlling faculties).

3. *Lokanirdeśa* (a treatment of the world arising out of *sāsrava dharmas*).

4. *Karmanirdeśa* (a treatment of *karma* causing repeated existence of sentient beings).

5. *Anuśayanirdeśa* (a treatment of 98 *anuśayas,* latent proclavities that condition the repeated existences).

6. *Pudgalamārganirdeśa* (a treatment of the Holy ones as fruits of *anāsrava,* i.e., *nirvāṇa*).

7. *Jñānanirdeśa* (a treatment of 10 knowledges that cause *nirvāṇa*).

8. *Samāpattinirdeśa* (a treatment of the meditiations that condition *anāsrava,* i.e, *nirvāṇa*).

9. *Pudgalaviniścaya* (Refutation of *Ātman* - theories of the *Sāmkhya,* the *Vaiśeṣika* and the *Vātsīputrīya* schools).

When we compare these topics with those of the *ADSPS* , along with the subject matter discussed in the two texts, we notice that,

1. The five precepts and the five misconducts discussed in the first chapter of the *ADSPS* are included in the 10

kuśalakarmapathas and in the 10 *akuśalakarmapathas* respectively in the sixth chapter of the *AK*. However in the first instance the *ADSPS*, following the manner of the *sūtra* gives details on precepts and laymen in its entire first chapter, where as the *AK* discusses the precepts breifly as a part of exposition on *karma*. The six *kāma*- heavens and the seventeen *rūpa* -heavens mentioned in the first chapter of the *ADSPS*, are detailed in the third chapter of the *AK*.

2. The topics discussed in the *ADSPS* chapters 2-10 and 15 are all included in the sixth chapter of the *AK* dealing with the *Āryas* of different stages of the Buddhist path, and the *Mārgas* (different stages leading to *Nirvāṇa*). The treatment of the subject matter in the *ADSPS*, however, is different, as one chapter is devoted to one topic of discussion only, the exposition of the doctrines in the text is done in a simple direct method of reclassification and eleboration of the *sūtras* on the basis of the authority of the *Āgamas* and the *Nikāyas*. The same topics, in the *AK* however, are treated in a more systematic manner and in a concise form. Thus chapter 6 of the *AK* mainly concentrates on two modes of abandoning the defilements, in keeping with the discussion on defilements in the previous chapter, that is the fifth chapter of the *AK*. The analysis of the *dharmas* in the *AK* is done by refering to critical standpoints, which is not seen in the *ADSPS*.

3. From the eleventh to the fourteenth chapter, the *ADSPS* explains various kinds of meditations attained by the adepts gradually during their progress in the Buddhist path. Thus chapter eleven deals with first four *dhyānas*, chapter twelve on the four boundless states of meditations, chapter thirteen on the four stages of formless meditation and chapter fourteen on the four *bhāvanāsamādhis*. The *AK*, deals with these types of *dhyānas* and their attainment in its eighth chapter with more classifications.

4. The *ADSPS* devotes its entire fifteen chapter on the

exposition of seven *bodhyaṅgas* only, while the later are briefly explained in the *AK* (VI. 71).

5. Each of the seventy-eight types of defilements (*Upakleśas*) is detailed in the sixteenth chapter of the *ADSPS*. The list comprises of the six *kleśamahābhumikās*, the two *akuśalamahābhūmikās* and the ten *parīttakleśamahābhūmikās*, and the eight *aniyatas* of the *AK* along with the other defilements mentioned in the *Nikāyas, Āgamas*, and *Vibhaṅga*. The 98 *anuśayas* described in the fifth *kośasthānas* also include some of the defilements mentioned in the *ADSPS*.

6. The twenty-two *indriyas* explained in the seventeenth chapter of the *ADSPS* are all included in the exposition on the *indriyas* in the second *kośasthāna* of the *AK*. However, the *ADSPS* follows the *ābhidhārmic* manner of the *Vibh.*, while the *AK* deals with the twenty -two *indriyas* and their relation with atoms, *caittas, cittaviprayuktas* etc.

7. The twelve *āyatanas* and the five *skandhas* explained in the eighteenth and the nineteenth chapter of the *ADSPS* respectively follows the line of exposition found in the *Vibh.* The same classification is discussed more critically in the first *kośasthāna* of the *AK*. The twentieth chapter of the *ADSPS* deals with the sixty-two *dhātus* in all, which are summarized in the *AKV*, pp.55-56. The *Ak* in the first *kośasthāna*, however eleborates the principal 18 *dhātus*, their characteristics, and more classifications of the *dhātus*.

1. On *Siksāpadas*

   Compared by Dietze :1984

2. On four *Srotāpatyaṅga*

C : *ADSPS*, 458b23

P : *SN.* IV.5; *DN.* I I I, 227; *DN.* 33.

3. On four *Avetyaprasāda*

C : *ADSPS* 460a17

P : *DN.* I I I, 227, *AN.* IV.106, *SN.* I.232.

S : *MV.*245, *AK.* VI. 73-74

4. On four *Śrāmaṇyaphala*

C : *ADSPS* 464c16

P : *DN.* 2,33, *Viśuddhimagga* 215,512; *SN.*V.2.

S : *AK.* IV, 50-51, 56

5. On four *Abhijñāpratipad*

C : *ADSPS* 465a22

P : *AN.* IV, 162-163, 166-169.

S : *AVS* 11

6. On four *Āryavaṃśa*

C : *ADSPS* 466b15

P : *Ariyavaṃsa Sutta* (*AN.* IV.28); *DN.* I I I. 224-5.

S : *AK.* VI. 7-9.

7. On four *Samyak Pradhānas*

C : *ADSPS* 467c23

P : *AN* 9.81 :

भिक्खु अनुप्पन्नानं पापकानं अकुसलानं धम्मानं अनुप्पादाय छन्दं जनेति वायमति विरियं आरभति चित्तं पग्गण्हाति पदहति; उप्पन्नानं पापकानं अकुसलानं धम्मानं पहानाय छन्दं जनेति वायमति विरियं आरभति पग्गण्हाति पदहति; अनुप्पन्नानं कुसलानं धम्मानं उप्पादाय छन्दं जनेति वायमति विरियं आरभति चितं पग्गण्हाति पदहाति; उप्पन्नानं कुसलानं धम्मानं ठितिया असम्मोसाय भिय्योभावाय वेपुल्लाय भावनाय पारिपूरिया

छन्दं जनेति वायमति विरियं आरभति चित्तं पग्गण्हाति पदहति। इमेसं खो. भिक्खवे पञ्चन्नं सिक्खादुब्बल्यानं पहानाय इमे चत्तारो सम्मप्पधाना भावेतव्वा ति।

S : *AVS* 14 :

(14) तत्र कतमानि भिक्षवश्चत्वारि सम्यक्प्रहाणानि ? इह भिक्षवो भिक्षुरनुत्पन्नानां पापकानामकुशलनां धर्माणमनुण्पादाय छन्दं जनयति व्यायच्छति वीर्यमारभते, चितं संप्रतिगृह्णाति, सम्यक् प्रणिदधाति। उत्पन्नानामकुशलानां धर्माणां प्रहाणायं छन्दं जनयति, व्यायच्छति, वीर्यमारभते, चितं प्रगृह्णाति सप्रंणिदधाति। अनुत्पन्नानां कुशलानां धर्माणामुत्पादाय छन्दं जनयति, व्यायच्छति, वीर्यमारभते, चितं प्रगृह्णाति, सम्यक् प्रणिदधाति। उत्पन्नानां कुशलानां धर्माणां स्थितये भावनायै असंमोषाय अपरिहाणाय भूयोमावाय वृद्धिविपुलतायै पारिपूर्यै छन्दं जनयति, व्यायच्छति, वीर्यमारभते चितं प्रतिगृह्णाति सम्यक् प्रणिदधाति। इमानि चत्वारि सम्यक्प्रहाणनि।

8. On four *Ṛddhipādas*

C : *ADSPS* 471c12

P : *AN* 9.9.1 ;

चत्तारो इद्धिपादा भावेतब्बा। कतमे चत्तारो इघ, भिक्खवे, भिक्खु छन्दसमाघिपधानसंखारसमन्नागतं इद्धिपादं भावेति, विरिय समाधि .. चितसमाधि .. मीमांसासमाधिपधानसंखरसमन्नागतं इद्धिपादं भावेति इमेसं खो, भिक्खवे, पञ्च न्नं सिक्खादुब्बल्यानं पहानाय इमे चत्तारो इद्धिपादा भावेतब्बा ति।

MN.I.103; *SN*.V.254; *AV*. IV. 309; *Vibh.* 216;
S : *DS* 46:

46. चत्वारः ऋद्धिपादाः। तद्यथा-छन्दसमाधिप्रहाणाय संस्कारसमन्वागत ऋद्धिपादः। एवं चित्तऋद्धिपादः। वीर्यऋद्धिपादः। मीमांसासमाधिप्रहाणाय संस्कार-समन्वागतऋद्धिपाद श्चेति ॥

9. On four *Smṛtyapasthānas*

C : *ADSPS*, 475c24
P : *AN* 9.7.2:

2. इमेसं, खो, भिक्खवे, पञ्चन्नं नीवरणानं पहानाय चन्तारो सतिपट्ठाना भावेतब्बा। कतमे चत्तारो? इघ, भिक्खवे, भिक्खु काये कायानुपस्सी विहरति आतापी सम्पजानो सतिमा विनेय्यं लोके अभिज्झादोमनस्सं वेदनासु .. पे॰ .. चित्ते .. घम्मेसु घम्मानुपस्सी विहरति आतापी सम्पजानो सतिमा विनेय्य लोके अभिज्झां दोमनस्सं। इमेसं खो, भिक्खवे, पञ्चन्नं नीवरणानं पहानाय इमे चत्तारो सतिपट्ठाना भावेतब्बा" ति।

Satipaṭṭhāna-sutta, DN. 22, MN. 10
S : *AVS* 13 :

(13) इह भिक्षवो भिक्षुरध्यात्मं काये कायानुदर्शी विहरति आतापी संप्रजानन् स्मृतिमान् विनीय लोके अभिध्यादौर्मनस्ये। बहिर्धा काये कायानुदर्शी विहरति ... आतापी संप्रजानन् अनुस्मृतिमान् विनीय लोके अभिव्ध्यादौर्मनस्ये। अध्यात्मवेदनासु बहिर्धावेदनासु अध्यात्मबहिर्धा वेदनासु वेदनानुदर्शी विहरति आतापी संप्रजानन् स्मृतिमान् विनीय लोके अभिध्यादौर्मनस्ये। अध्यात्मचित्ते बहिर्धाचित्ते अध्यात्मबहिर्धा चित्तानुदर्शी विहरति आतापी संप्रजानन् स्मृतिमान् विनीय लोके अभिघ्यादौर्मनस्ये। अध्यात्मधर्मेषु बहिर्धाधर्मेषु अध्यात्मबहिर्धाधर्मेषु धर्मानुदर्शी विहरति आतापी संप्रजानन् स्मृतिमान् विनीय लोके अभिघ्यादौर्मनस्ये। इतीमोनि चत्वारि स्मृत्युपस्थानाानि।

10. On four *Āryastyas*

C : *ADSPS*, 479b24
P : *Vibh.* Ch. IV
S : *AK.* : *AVS* 6 : *DS* 21

11. On four *Dhyānas*

C : *ADSPS*, 482a26
P : *MN* Nos. 181, 25-28, 32-35, 182, 2-6, 10-14
S : *AVS* 9 :

[9] तत्र भिक्षवश्चत्वारि ध्यानानि कतमानि ? इह भिक्षवो भिक्षुर्विविक्तं कामैः विविक्तं पापकैरकुशलैर्धर्मैः सवितर्कं सविचारं विवेकजं प्रीतिसुखं प्रथमं ध्यानमुपसंपद्य बिहरति। स बितर्कविचाराणां व्युपशमादध्यात्मसंप्रसादाच्चेतस एकोतिभावादवितर्कमविचारं समाधिजं प्रीतिसुखं द्वितीयं ध्यानमुपसंपद्य विहरति। स प्रीतेर्विरागादुपेक्षको बिहरति, स्मृतः संप्रजन्यं च (संप्रजानन्) सुखं कायेन प्रतिसंवेदयते–यत्तदार्या आचक्षते उपेक्षकः स्मृतिमान् सुखविहारी–तृतीयं ध्यानमुपसंपद्य विहरति। स सुखस्य च प्रहाणाद्दुःखस्य च प्रहाणात् पूर्वमेव सौमनस्यदौर्मनस्ययोरस्तंगमाद (10a) दुःखासुखमुपेक्षास्मृतिपरिशुद्धं चतुर्थ ध्यान मुपसंपद्य विहरति॥ इमानि भिक्षवश्चत्त्वारि ध्यानांनि॥

12. On four *Apramāṇas*
C : *ADSPS*, 485a26
P : *Vibh* ; *MN.* No. 38, 20-30; *DN*
S : *AK.*
cf four Brahmavihāras in *AVS* 10:

[10] तत्र कतमे चत्वारो ब्रह्मविहाराः ? इह भिक्षवो भिक्षुर्मैत्रीसहगतेन चित्तेन अवैरेण असंपन्नेन अव्याबाधेन बिपुलेन महद्गतेन अप्रमाणेन सुभावितेन एकाद्रिसमं विमुच्य स्फुरित्वा उपसंपद्य बिहरति, तथा द्वितीयम्, तथा तृतीयम्, तथा चतुर्थम्, इति ऊर्ध्वमधस्तिर्यक् सर्वशः सर्वावन्तमिमं लोकं मैत्रीसहगतेन चित्तेन अवैरेण असंपन्नेन अव्याबाधेन विपुलेन महद्गतेन अद्वयेन अप्रमाणेन सुभावितेन एकां दिशमधिमुच्य स्फुरित्वा उपसंपद्य विहरति। एवं करुणासहगतेन मुदितासहगतेन, उपेक्षासहगतेन चित्तेन अवैरेण असंपन्नेन अव्याबाधेन विपुलेन महद्गतेन अद्वयेन अप्रमाणेन सुभावितेन एकां दिशमधिमुच्य स्फुरित्वा उपसंपद्य विहरति। इमे चत्वारो ब्रह्मबिहाराः॥

13. On four *Ārūpya*
C : *ADSPS*, 488b19
P : *MN* No.436,18-26; *Vibh.*
S : *AK.* VIII.2-6.
14. On four *Bhāvanāsamādhi*

C : *ADSPS*, 489a29
P : *DN.*I I I.222; *AN.*I I.44
S : *AVS* 12; *AK.* VI I I.27.

15. On seven *Bodhyaṅga*

C : *ADSPS*, 491b8
P : *MN.* I I.12,14-23; *DN.*I I.120; *Vibh.* 10, p.9.18.
S : *AVS* 18: *AK.* VI.67

16. On *Kṣudrakavastu*

C : *ADSPS,* 494c1
P : *Vibh.* 17.2.5-23, 26-45; 17.3.49-52; 58-61
S : *AK.* I I.27 with *AKB*; AK.V. with *AKB.*

17. On twenty-two *Indriyas*

C : *ADSPS* 498b13
P : *Vibh.* V
S : *Avs.*7, *AK.* I I.

18. On twelve *Āyatanas*

C : *ADSPS,*499c25
P : *Vibh.* I I
S : *AVS* 4; *AK.* I

19. On five *Skandhas*

C : *ADSPS,* 500c26
P : *Vibh.* I.
S : *AVS* I.*AK.* I.

20. On various *Dhātus*

C : *ADSPS,* 501b24
P : *MN.* I I I.61 explains forty-one *dhātus*
S : *AK.* I I, AKV. p.

21. On *Pratītyasamutpāda*

C : *ADSPS,* 505a9
P : *Vibh.* VI; *AN.* *V.*214,10-17; I II. 32, 2-3; *DN.* I I. 62, 38-63; I I. 63, 18-26.
S : *AVS* 5; *AK.* I I I. 20-27, *AKV*, pp. 435-448.

6. *ABHIDHARMA-DHARMASKANDHA-PĀDAŚĀSTRA* : SANSKRIT-CHINESE ENGLISH VOCABULARY

I. *Śikṣāpadāni* 學處

Precepts

Pañca bhayāni
wu- pu 五怖畏
Five misconducts

1. *Prāṇātipāta*
sha- sheng 殺生
Taking life

2. *Adattādāna*
pu-yu-chu 不與取
Taking what is not given

3. *Kāmamithyācāra*
Yü- na-hsing 欲邪行
Lying

4. *Mṛṣāvāda*
hsü-k'uang-yü 虛誑語
Lying

5. *Surāmaireyamadyapramādasthāna*
yü- wei- chu- chiu- fang- yi- ch'u 飲諸酒放逸處
Taking intoxicants that causes indolence

Pañcaśilāni
wu- chiai 五 戒

Five Moral Rules

1. *Prāṇātipātāt prativirati*
li-sha- sheng' 離殺生
Abstaining from taking life

2. *Adattādānād prativirati* 離不與取
   li-pu-yü-chu
   Abstaining from what is not given

3. *Kāmamithyācārād prativirati* 離欲邪行
   li- yü-na-hsing
   Abstaining from lying

4. *Mṛṣāvādād prativirati* 離虛誑語
   li-hsu- k'uang-yü
   Abstaining from lying

5. *Surāmaireyamadyapramādasthānat prativirati* 離飲諸酒放逸處
   li-yin- chu-chiu-fang-yi-ch'u
   Abstaining from the use of intoxicants

Upāsaka 鄔波索迦
wu- p'o-so-chia
Layman

1. *Śikṣāsu ekadeśakārī* 能學一分
   neng-hsueh-yi-fen
   Layman observing one of the five precepts

2. *Śikṣāsu pradeśakārī* 能學小分
   neng-hsueh-hsiao-fen
   Layman observing two of the five precepts

3. *Śikṣāsu Yadbhūyaskārī* 爲能學多分
   wei-neng-hsueh- tuo- fen
   Laymen observing three of the five precepts

4. *Śikṣāsu aparipūrṇakāri*
   Layman observing four of the five precepts

5. *Śikṣāsu paripūrṇakārī* 能學滿分。
   neng-hsueh-man-fen
   Layman observing five precepts

6. *Pañcabhir dharmaiḥ samanvāgatāḥ upāsakāḥ* 成就五法鄔波索迦
   ch'eng- chiu-wu-fa-wu-p'o-so-chia

Layman who has attained five *dharmas*

7. *Daśabhir dharmaiḥ samanvāgatā upāsakāḥ*
ch'eng-chiu- shih-fa- wu-p'o-so-chia
Laymen who has attained ten *dharmas*

成就十法鄔波索迦。

8. *Pañcadaśabhir dharmaiḥ samanvāgatāḥ upāsakāḥ*
ch'eng-chiu-shih-wu-fa-wu-p'o-so-chia
Laymen who has attained fifteen *dharmas*

就十五法鄔波索迦。

9. *Aṣṭabhir dharmaiḥ samanvāgatāḥ Upāsakāḥ*
ch'eng-chiu-pa-fa-wu-p'o-so-chia

成就八法鄔波索迦。

10. *Soḍaśabhir dharmaih samanvāgatā upāsakāḥ*
ch'eng-chiu-shih-liu-fa- wu-p'o-so-chia
Layman who has attained sixteen *dharmas*

成就十六一法鄔波索迦

11. *Caturviṃśatya dharmaiḥ samanvāgatā upāsakāḥ*
ch'eng-chiu-erh-shih-tse-fa-wu--p'o-so-chia
Layman who has attained twenty four *dharmas*

成就二十四法鄔波索迦。

12. *Vimśatyā dharmaiḥ samanvāgatāḥ Upāsakāḥ*
ch'eng-chiu-erh-shih-fa-wu-p'o-so-chia
Layman who has attained twenty *dharmas*

成就二十法。

13. *Trimśatā dharmaiḥ samanvāgatā Upāsakāḥ*
ch'eng-chiu-san-shih-fa-wu-p'o-so-chia
Layman who has attained thirty *dharmas*

成就三十法

14. *Catvārimśatā dharmaih samanvāgatā Upāsakāḥ*
ch'eng-chiu- tse-shih-fa-wu-p'o-so-chia
Layman who has attained forty *dharmas*

成就四十法，

Pañcopāsakasya śikṣāpadāni
Five moral rules for layman

1. *Yāvajjīvam prāṇātipātād viratiḥ.*
nai-chih-ling-chung-yüan- li-sha-shang
Abstaining from taking life for life time

。乃至命終遠離殺生

2. *Yāvajjīvam adattādānat viratiḥ*
nai- chih-ling-chung-li-pu-yu-chu

乃至命終。離不與取。

Abstaining from taking life for life time

3. *Yāvajjīvam kāmamithyācārat viratiḥ* 乃至命終。離欲邪行。
nai-chih-ling-chung-li-yü-na-hsing
Abstaining from unchastity for life time

4. *Yāvajjivam mṛṣāvādāt viratiḥ* 乃至命終。離虛誑語
nai-chih-ling-chung-li-hsü-k'uang-yü
Abstaining from lying for life time

5. *Yāvajjīvam surāmaireyamadyapramādasthānad viratiḥ* 乃至命終。離飲諸酒諸放逸處。
nai-chih-ling-chung-li-yin-chu-chiu-chu- fang-yi-ch'u
Abstaining from the use of intoxicants for life-time.

Adattādāyikah 不與取者
pu-yu-chu-che
One who takes what is not given to him
Kāmamithyācārika 欲邪行者
yü-na-hsing-che
One who is unchaste
mṛṣāvādika 虛誑語者
hsü-kuang-yü-che
One who lies
Surāmireyamadyapramāda sthānika 飲味諸酒放逸處者
yin-wei-chu-chiu-fang-yi-ch'u-che
One who takes intoxicants etc.

II. *Srotāpatyaṅgāṇi* 預流支
yü-liu-chih
Conditions of attaining the stream

Catvāri srotāpatyaṅgāni
Four conditions of attaining the stream

1. *Satpuruṣasaṃsevā* 親近善士
ch'in-chin-shan-shih
Companionship with good persons

2. *Saddharmaśravaṇam* 聽聞正法。
t'ing-wen-cheng-fa
Hearing to good law

3. *Yoniśo manaskāra* 如理作意。
ru-li-tso-yi
Wise Reflection

4. *Dhammānudharmapratipatti* 法隨法行。
fa-sui-fa-hsing
Living in conformity with the law

III. *Avetya prasādāḥ* *cheng-ching* 證淨 Attainments of Faith and Purity

Catvāri avetyaprasādāni
tse-cheng-ching
Four attainments of faith and purity

1. *Buddhe avetyaprasāda* 佛證淨
fo-cheng-ching
Faith relating to the *aśaikṣa dharmas* of the Buddha

2. *Dharme avetyaprasāda* 法證淨
fa-cheng-ching
Faith relating to the *Dharma*, i.e., four Noble truths

3. *Saṅghe avetyaprasāda* 僧證淨
seng-cheng-ching
Faith relating to the *Saṅgha*

4. *Āryakāntāni śīlāni* 聖所愛戒。
sheng-suo-ai-chiai
Purity dear to the saint
Cf. four *aṅgas* of the learners

IV. *Śrāmaṇyaphalāni*
sha-man-kuo 沙門果
Fruits of Religious Life

Catvāri śrāmaṇyaphalāni
tse sha-men-kuo 四沙門果
Four Fruits of Religious Life

1. *Srotāpattiphala*
   yü-liu-kuo 預流果
   Fruit of stream-winning

2. *Sakṛdāgāmiphala*
   yi-lai-kuo 一來果
   fruit of Once-returning

3. *Anāgāmiphala*
   pu-yuan-lai 不還果
   fruit of no-returning

4. *Arhattaphala*
   a-lo-han-kuo 阿羅漢果
   Fruit of the Perfect One

V. *Abhijñāpratipad*
t'ung-hsing 通行
Progress to Deliverance

Cattāri abhijñā padāni
tse-tung-hsing
Four modes of progress

1. *Duḥkha pratipad dhandāvijñā*
   k'u-pien-t'ung-hsing 苦遲通行
   Painful progress with slow comprehension

2. *Duḥkha pratipad kṣiprāvijñā*
   k'u-se-t'ung-hsing 苦速通行

Painful progress with quick comprension

3. *Sukhā pratipad dhandāvijñā*
le-pien-t'ung-hsing
Pleasant progress with slow compreshion

4 *Sukhā pratipad kṣiprāvijñā*
le-se-t'ung-hsing
Pleasant progress with quick comprehsion

VI. *Āryavamśa*
sheng-chung
Noble Lineage

Catvārāh āryavamśāh
tse-sheng-chung
Four Classes of the Buddha's disciples

1. *Cīvarasantuṣṭisvabhāva*
yi-fu-an-chu-sheng-chung
To be content with clothing

2. *Piṇḍapātasantuṣṭisvabhāva*
yin-shih- an-chu...sheng......chung
To be content with food

3. *Śayanāsanasantuṣṭisvabhāvah*
wu-chu......an-chu.......sheng-chung
To be content with bed and seat

4. *Prahānabhāvanāramatā*
yu-tuan-ai-le-an-chu-ku- sheng-chung
To take delight in Extinction meditation

VII. *Samyakpradhānāni*
Cheng-sheng
Right strivings

Catvāri samyakpradhānāni

tse-cheng-sheng
Four Right Striving

1. *Utpannānām pāpakānām akuṣalānām dharmānām prahāṇāya chhandam janayati vyāyacchati vīryam āravate, cittam pragṛhṇāti cittam praṇidadhāti.*

(A *bhikṣu*) engenders wish, makes effort, arouses energy, exerts the mind, strives for the abandoning of evil bad states that have arisen.

2. *Anutpannānām pāpakānām aksuśalānām dharmānām anutpādāya chandam janayati, vyāyacchati, vīryamāravate, cittam pragṛhṇāti,cittam praṇidadhāti.*

(A *bhikṣu*) engenders wish, makes effort, arouses energy, exerts the mind, strives for the abandoning of evil bad states that have not arisen.

3. *Anutpannānām kuśalānām dharmānam utpādāya chandam janayati, vyāyacchati, vīryam āravate, cittam pragṛhṇāti, cittam praṇidhati*

(A *bhikṣu*) engenders wish, makes effort, arouses energy, exerts the mind, strives for the arising of good states that have not arisen.

4. *Utpannānām kuśalānām dharmānām sthitaye asammoṣāya bhāvanāyai paripuryai bhūyobhāvāya vṛddhi vipulatāyai chandam janayati vyāyaccati, vīryam āravate cittam pragṛhṇāti, cittam praṇidadhati* A *bhikusu* ..... for maintaining the good states that have arisen.

VIII. *Ṛddhipādāḥ*
shen-tsu
Bases of power

神足。

1. *Chandasamādhi*
Concentration of Desire

欲三摩地勝行成就神足。

2. *Vīryasamādhi* 勤三摩地勝行成就神足。
   Concentration of Energy

3. *Cittasamādhi* 心三摩地勝行成就神足,
   Concentration of Mind

4. *Mīmāmsāsamādhi* 觀三摩地勝行成就神
   Concentration of Investigation

IX. *Smṛtyupasthānāni*
nien-chu 念住
Base of Mindfulness

Catvāri smṛtyupasthānāni
tse-nien-chu 四念住
Four Bases of Mindfulness

1. *Kāyasmṛtyupasthāna shen-nien-chu* 身念住
   Mindfulness with regard to body
2. *Vedanāsmṛtyupasthāna shou-nien-chu* 受念住
   Minfulness with regard to feeling
3. *Cittasmṛtyupasthāna hsin-nien-chu* 心念住
   Mindfulness with regard to mind
4. *Dharmasmṛtyupasthāna fa-nien-chu* 法念住
   Mindfulness with regard to phenomena

X. *Āryasatya*
sheng-li 聖諦
Noble Truth

Catvari āryasatyāni
tse sheng-ti 四聖諦
Four Noble Truths

1. *Duḥkha āryasatya* 苦聖諦

k'u-sheng-ti
The Noble Truth of Suffering

2. *Duḥkhasamudaya āryasatya* 苦集聖諦
k'u -ch'i-sheng-ti
The Noble Truth of the cause of suffering

3. *Duḥkhanirodha āryasatya* 苦滅聖諦
k'u-mieh-sheng-ti
The Noble Truth of the cessation of suffering

4. *Mārgasatya* 苦滅道聖諦
k'u-mieh-tao-sheng-ti
The Noble Truth of the way leading to cessation of suffering

Eight fold Noble Path 八支聖道
pa-chih-sheng-tao

XI. *Dhyānāni*
ching-hsü 靜慮
Meditative Absorptions

Catvāri rūpadhyāni 四天道
tse-tian-tao
Four Absorptions on visible spheres (*rūpadhyāna*)

1. *Prathamam dhyānam* 初靜慮
chu-ching-hsü
Attainment of first Absorption

2. *Dvitiyam dhyānam* 第二靜慮
ti-erh-ching-hsü
Attainment of Second Absorption

3. *Tritiyam Dhyānam* 第三靜慮
ti-san-ching-hsü
Attainment of first Absorption

4. *Caturtham Dhyānam*

第四靜慮 *ti-tse-ching-hsü*
Attainment of first Absorption

XII. *Apramānāni* 無量
wu-liang
Immeasurables

Catvāri apramāṇāni
tse wu-liang
Four Immeasurables

1. *Maitrī* 慈
   tz'u
   Loving kindness
2. *Karuṇā* 悲
   pei
   Compassion
3 *Muditā* 喜
   hsi
   Sympathetic joy
4. *Upekṣā* 捨
   she
   Equanimity

XIII. *Ārūpyāni* 無色
wu-se
Formless Spheres

Catvāri Ārūpyāṇi
tse wu-se 四無色
Four Formless Spheres

1. 空無邊處 *Ākāśānantyāyatana*
   k'ung-wu-pien- ch'u

Sphere of Boundless Space

2. *Vijñānāntyāyatana* 識無邊處
shih-wu-pien-ch'u
Sphere of Boundless Consciousness

3. *Ākiñcanyāyatana* 無所有處
wu-suo-yu-ch'u
Sphere of Nothingness

4. *Nāsaṃjñānāpyasaṃjñāyatana* 非想非非想處
fei-hsiang-fei-fei-hsiang-ch'u
Sphere of Neither-Notion-Nor- Absence of Notion

XIV. *Bhāvanāsamādhayaḥ* 修定
hsiu-ting
Cultivations of Absorption

Catasra bhāvanāsamādhayaḥ
tse-hsiu-ting 四修定
Four Cultivations of Absorption

1. *Samādhibhāvanā dṛṣṭadharmasukhavihārāya* 得現法樂住修定
te-hsien-fa-le-chu-hsiu-ting
Absorption leading to attainment of happiness in this world

2. *Samādhibhāvana Jñānadarśanapratilābhāya* 得殊勝智見修定
te-shu-sheng-chih-chien-hsiu- ting
Absorption leading to the attainment of the seeing of knowledge

3. *Samādhibhāvanā prajñā - pratilambhāya* 得勝分別慧修定
te-sheng-fen-pieh-hui-hsiu-ting
Absorption leading to the attainment of wisdom

4. *Samādhibhāvana Kāmarāgaprahāṇāya* 得諸漏永盡修定
te-chu-lou-yung-chin-hsiu-ting
Absorption leading to the destruction of sensuous

lust and attachment

XV. *Bodhyaṅgāni*
chueh-chih 覺支
Factors of Enlightenment

Sapta Bodhyaṅgāni
ch'i chueh-chih 七覺支
Seven Factors of Enlightenment

1. *Smṛti - saṃbodhyaṅga* 念覺支
   nien-chueh-chih
   Mindfulness Enlightenment factor

2. *Dharmavicaya - saṃbodhyaṅga* 法覺支
   fa-chueh-chih
   Truth-investigation Enlightenment - factor

3. *Vīrya - saṃbodhyaṅga* 精進覺支。
   ch'ing-chin-chueh-chih
   Energy Enlightenment - factor

4. *Prīti - saṃbodhyaṅga* 喜覺支
   shan - chueh - chih
   Rapture Enlightenment - factor

5. *Praśrabdhi - saṃbodhyaṅga* 輕安覺支
   ch'ing - an - chueh - chih
   Tranquility Enlightenment - factor

6. *Samādhi - saṃbodhyaṅga* 定覺支。
   ting - chueh - chih
   Concentration Enlightenment - factor

7. *Upekṣā - saṃbodhyaṅga* 捨覺支。
   she - chueh - chih
   Equanimity Enlightenment - factor

XVI. *Kṣudrakavastu*
tsa-shih

Miscellaneous Matters
Mental faculties

1. *Rāga t'an* Attachment
2. *Dveṣa ch'en* Hatred
3. *Moha ch'ih* Delusion
4. *Krodha fen* Fury
5. *Upanāha hen* Enmity
6. *Mrakṣa fu* Hypocricy
7. *Pradāśa nao* Vexation
8. *Īrṣyā chi* Envy
9. *Mātsarya chien* Parsimony
10. *Śāṭhya k'uang* Deception
11. *Māyā ch'an* Duplicity
12. *Āhrikya wu-ts'an* Absence of shame
13. *Anapatrāpya wu-kuei* Absence of fear of blame
14. *Māna man* Conceit
15. *Atimāna kuo-man* Excessive conceit
16. *Mānātimāna man-kuo-man* Inordinate conceit
17. *Asmimāna wo-man* Self-conceit
18. *Adhimāna tseng-shang-man* Over-estimating conceit
19. *Ūnamāna pei-man* Self-disrespect conceit
20. *Mithyāmāna hsieh-man* False conceit
21. *Mada chueh* Pride
22. *Pramāda fang-i* Idlessness
23. *āo* (?) Proud

貪瞋癡忿恨覆惱嫉慳誑 諂無慚無愧慢
過慢慢過慢我慢
增上慢卑慢 邪慢憍放逸傲

24. *fen* (?) Zealous
25. *Chiao wang* (?) Pretending
26. *Kuei* (*cha*) Crafty
27. *Naimittakatā hsien-hsiang* signifying
28. *Nispesikata chi-mo* defamation
29. *Lābhena lābha nijigīsanata* Seeking gain with gain *i-li-ch'iu-li*
30. *Pāpicchatā e-yü* Evil wish
31. *Mahicchatā ta-yü* Wish for the most
32. *Atricchatā hsien-yü* Wish for the best
33. *Pu-hsi-tsu* (?) Dissatisfaction
34. *Pu-kung-ching* (?) Disrespect
35. *Daurvacasyata Ch'i-e-yen* Contumacy
36. *Pāpamitratā lo-e-yu* Having evil friend
37. *Akṣānti pu-jen* Impatience
38. *Tan-shih-pien-tan-shih* (?) Addicted to pleasure
39. *Jan-tan* Affected by Attachment
40. *Adharmarāga fei-fa* Attachment to disregard
41. *Cha-tan* (?) Attachment to wealth
42. *Pāparāga e-t'an* Attachment to evil
43. *Satkāyadṛṣṭi yu-sheng-chien* Personality belief.
44. *Śāsvatadṛṣṭi yu-chien* viewpoint of Eternalism
45. *Uccedadṛṣṭi wu-yu-chien* View-point of nihilism
46. *Kāmarāga t'an-yu* -Attachment to desire
47. *Vyāpāda Ch'en-hai* Ill-will
48. *Styāna hun-ch'en* Torpidmindedness

憤發憍妄詭詐現相激磨以利

求利

惡欲大欲顯欲不喜足下恭敬起惡言[illegible]　惡友不忍

耽嗜遍耽嗜染貪非法。貪著貪惡　貪有身見有見

無有見　貪欲瞋恚惛沈

49. *Middha shui-mien* Drowsiness
50. *Auddhatya tiao-chu* Dissipation
51. *Kaukṛtya* (*tso-yi*) Remorse
52. *Vicikitsā i*-Doubt
53. *Arati pu-lo* Tedium
54. *Vijṛimbhikā p'in-shen-ch'ien-ch'u* Restlessness
55. *Bhukta samatā she-pu-t'iao-sing* After-Meal drowsiness
56. *Cetaso līnatva hsin-mei-lieh-hsing* Mental sluggishness
57. *Nānātva-samjñā chung-chung-hsiang* Notion of variety
58. *Ayoniśo manaskāra pu-tsoyi* Wrong judgement
59. *Dausṭhulya fu chung* Heaviness
60. *Ti-t'u* (Rudeness)
61. *Śringi t'ao* Foppery
62. *Tintilaka yen* Presumption
63. *Anarjavatā pu-ho-ju-hsing* Non-straightness
64. *Amārdavatā pu-t'iao-jou-hsing* Non-gentleness
65. *Asabhāgānuvartana pu-shun-ting-lei* Discourteous living
66. *Kāmavitarka yü-hsin* Reflection connected with desire
67. *Vyāpadavitarka wei-hsin* Reflection connected with Ill-will.
68. *Vihiṃsāvitarka hai-hsin* Reflection connected with Harmfulness
69. *Jñativitarka ch'in-li-hsing* Reflection about relatives

70. *Janapadavitarka kuo-t'u-hsin* Reflection about one's districts 國土尋

71. *Amaravitarka pu-tse-hsin* Reflection about how not to die 不死尋

72. *Apamanyana pratisaṃyukta vitarka ling-mien-hsin* Reflection connected with insulting others 陵蔑尋

73. *Kulodayapratisaṃyukta vitarka chia-tsu-hsin* Reflection with one's birth in excellent clan 假族尋

74. *chou śoka* Grief 愁

75. *Parideva pei* Lamentation 悲

76. *Duḥkha k'u* Sorrow 苦

77. *Daurmanasya yu* Mental pain 憂

78. *Upāyāsa jao nao* Despair 擾惱。

XVII. *Indriyāni* *ken* Controlling Faculties 根

Dvāvimśati indriyāni
erh-shih-erh-ken 二十二根
Twenty two Controlling faculties

1. *Cakṣurindriya*
yen-ken 眼根、
Controlling faculty of Eye

2. *Śrotrendriya*
erh-ken 耳根。
Controlling faculty of Ear

3. *Ghrāṇendriya*
p'i-ken 鼻根。
Controlling faculty of Nose

4. *Jiḥvendriya* 舌根。
she-ken
Controlling faculty of Tongue

5. *Kāyendriya* 身根。
shen-ken
Controlling faculty of Body

6. *Manendriya* 意根。
yi-ken
Controlling faculty of Mind

7. *Strīrindriya* 女根。
nu-ken
Controlling faculty of Faminity

8. *Puruṣendriya* 男根。
nan-ken
Controlling faculty of Masculinity

9. *Jīvitendriya* 命根。
ling-ken
Controlling faculty of Vitality

10. *Sukhendriya* 樂根。
lo-ken
Controlling faculty of Pleasure

11. *Duḥkhendriya* 苦根。
k'u-ken
Controlling faculty of Bodily Pain

12. *Soumanasyendriya* 喜根。
hsi-ken
Controlling faculty of Mental Pleasure

13. *Daurmanasyendriya* 憂根。
yu-ken
Controlling faculty of Mental Pain

14. *Upekṣendriya*

She-ken 捨根
Controlling faculty of Confidence

15. *Śraddhendriya* 信根
Hsin-ken
Controlling faculty of Confidence

16. *Vīryendriya* 精進根
Ch'ing-chin-ken
Controlling faculty of Energy

17. *Smṛtīndriya* 念根
nian-ken
Controlling faculty of Mindfulness

18. *Samādhīndriya* 定根
ting-ken
Controlling faculty of Concentration

19. *Jñānendriya* 慧根
hui-ken
Controlling faculty of Wisdom

20. *Anajñātāmajñāsyāmīndriya* 未知當知根
mo-chih-tang-chih-ken
Controlling Faculty of the assurance ; 'I shall know what I did not yet know'

21. *Ajñendriya* 已知根
yichih-ken
Controlling Faculty of Highest knowledge

22. *Ājñātāvīndriya* 具知根
chü-chih-ken
Controlling Faculty of Final Enlightenment

XVIII. *Āyatanāni* 處
Ch'u
Bases

1. *Cakṣurindriya* 眼處

yen-ch'u
Eye (visual organ)

2. *Śroṭrāyàtana* 耳處
erh-ch'u
Ear (auditory organ)

3. *Ghrāṇāyatana* 鼻處
p'i-ch'u
Nose (olfactory organ)

4. *Jihvāyatana* 舌處
she-ch'u
Tongue (gustatory organ)

5. *Kāyāyatana* 身處
shen-ch'u
Body (tactile organ)

6. *Manāyatana* 意處
yi-ch'u
Mind (consciousness)

7. *Rūpāyatana* 色處
se-ch'u
Material existence

8. *Śabdāyatana* 聲處
sheng-ch'u
Sound

9. *Gandhāyatana* 香處
hsiang-ch'u
Smell

10. *Rasāyatana* 味處
wei-ch'u
Taste

11. *Sparśāyatana* 觸處
ch'u-ch'u

Body - impression

12. *Dharmāyatana* 法處
fa-ch'u
Mind object

XIX. *Skandhāni* 蘊
yün
Aggregates

Pañca skandhāni 五蘊
Five *skandhas*

1. *Rūpaskandha* 色蘊
se-yün
Form - aggregate

2. *Vedanāskandha* 受蘊
shou-yün
Feeling-aggregate

3. *Samjñāskandha* 想蘊
hsiang-yün
Notion-aggregate

4. *Saṃskāraskandha* 行蘊
hsing-yün
Volition-aggregate

5. *Vijñānaskandha* 識蘊
shih-yün
Consciousness-aggregate

XX. *Nānādhātu* 多界
tuo-chieh
Various elements

1. *Cakṣurdhātu*

yen-chieh 眼界
Eye element

2. *Rūpadhātu* 色界
se-chieh
Material existence element

3. *Cakṣurvijñānadhātu* 眼識界
yen-shih-chieh
Eye-consciousness element

4. *Śrotradhātu* 耳界
erh-chieh
Ear-element

5. *Śabdadhātu* 聲界
sheng-chieh
Sound-element

6. *Śrotravijñānadhātu* 耳識界
erh-shih-chieh
Ear-consciousness element

7. *Ghrāṇadhātu* 鼻界
p'i-chieh
Nose-element

8. *Gandhadhātu* 香界
hsiang-chieh
Smell-element

9. *Ghrāṇavijñānadhātu* 鼻識界
p'i-shih-chieh
Nose-consciousness element

10. *Jihvādhātu* 舌界
she-chieh
Tongue-element

11. *Rasadhātu* 味界
wei-chieh
Taste-element

12. *Jiḥvāvijñānadhātu* 舌識界
she-shih-chieh
Tongue-consciousness element

13. *Kāyadhātu* 身界
shen-chieh
body-element

14. *Spraṣṭavyadhātu* 觸界
ch'u-chieh
Touch-element

15. *Kāyavijñānadhātu* 身識界
shen-shih-chieh
Body-consciousness element

16. *Manodhātu* 意界
yi-chieh
Mind-element

17. *Dharmadhātu* 法界
fa-chieh
Mind-object element

18. *Manovijñānadhātu* 意識界
yi-shih-chieh
Mind-consciousness element

19. *Pṛthvīdhātu* 地界
ti-chieh
Earth-element

20. *Āpodhātu* 水界
shui-chieh
Water-element

21. *Tejodhātu* 火界
huo-chieh
Fire-element

22. *Vāyudhātu* 風界
feng-chieh
Wind-element

23. *Ākaśadhātu* 空界
k'ung-chieh
Space-element

24. *Vijñānadhātu* 識界。
shih-chieh
Consciousness-elements

25. *Kāmadhātu* 欲界。
yü-chieh
Sensuality-element

26. *Vyāpādadhātu* 恚界。
wei-chieh
Ill-will element

27. *Vihiṃsādhātu* 害界
hai-chieh
Harmfulness element

28. *Naiṣkramyadhātu* 無欲界
wei-yü-chieh
Non-sensuality element

29. *Avyāpādadhātu* 無恚界。
wu-wei-chieh
Non-ill-will element

30. *Avihiṃsādhātu* 無害界。
wu-hai-chieh
Non-harmfulness element

31. *Sukhadhātu* 樂界。
lo-chieh
Happiness-element

32. *Duḥkhadhātu* 苦界。
k'u-chieh
Suffering-element

33. *Saumanasyadhātu* 喜界。
hsi-chieh
Mental pleasure-element

34. *Daurmanasyadhātu* 憂界。
yu-chieh
Mental pain-element

35. *Upekṣādhātu* 捨界。
she-chieh
Indifference-element

36. *Avidyā dhātu* 無明界
wu-ming-chieh
Ignorance-element

37. *Vedanādhatu* 受界
shou-chieh
Feeling-element

38. *Saṃjñādhātu* 想界。
hsiang-chieh
Notion-element

39. *Saṃskāradhātu* 行界
hsing-chieh
Volition-element

40. *Vijñānadhātu* 識界
shih-chieh
Consciousness-element

41. *Kāmadhātu* 欲界
yü-chieh
Sensuality-element

42. *Rūpadhātu* 色界
se-chieh
Form-element

43. *Ārūpyadhātu* 無色界
wu-se-chieh
Formless-element

44. *Nirodhadhātu* 滅界
mieh-chieh
Extinction-element

45. *Atītadhātu* 過去界
guo-ch'u chieh
Past element

46. *Anāgatadhātu* 未來界
mo-lai-chieh
Future element

47. *Pratyutpannadhātu* 現在界
hsien-tsai-chieh
Present element

48. *Hīnadhātu*
mo-lai-chieh
Inferior element

49. *Madhyamadhātu*
chung-chieh
Middle element

50. *Praṇītadhātu*
miao-chieh
Excellent element

51. *Kuśaladhātu*
shan-chieh
Good element

52. *Akuśaladhātu*
pu-shan-chieh
Bad element

53. *Avyākṛtadhātu*
wu-chi-chieh
Neutral element

54. *Śaikṣadhātu*
hsueh-chieh
Learner element

55. *Aśaikṣadhātu*
wu-hsueh-chieh
Non-learner element

56. *Naivaśaikṣa-nāśaikṣadhātu*
fei-hsueh-fei-wu-hsueh-chieh
non-learner element

57. *Sāsravadhātu*
yu-pien-chieh
Impure elements

58. *Anāsravadhātu*
wu-lou-chieh
Pure element

59. *Saṃskṛtadhātu*
yu-wei-chieh
Conditioned element

60. *Asaṃskṛtadhātu*
wu-wei-chieh
Unconditioned element

中界 妙界 善界 不善界 無記界 學界 無學界 有漏界

非學非無學界

無漏界 有爲界 無爲界

XXI. *Pratītyasamutpāda* *yüan-ch'u* Dependant Orgination

Avidyā pratyayā saṃskārāh wu-ming Yüan hsing

Through ignorance are conditioned the volitions
Saṃskārapratyayam vijñānam hsing yuan shih

Through volition is conditioned consciouoness

Vijñānapratyayam nāmarūpam shih yüan ming se

Through consciousness is conditioned mental and physical existence

Nāmarūpapratyayam saḍāyatanam ming se yüan liu ch'u

Through the mental and physical existence are conditioned the six bases

Saḍāyatanapratyayāḥ sparsāḥ liu ch'u yüan chu

Through the six bases is conditioned the contact

Sparśapratyayāḥ vedanā chu yüan shou

Through contact is conditioned Feeling

Vedanāpratyayā tṛṣṇā shou yüan ai

Through Feeling is conditioned Craving

Tṛṣṇāpratyayā upādānam ai yüan chu

Through Craving is conditioned Clinging

Upādānapratyayā bhava chu yüan yu

Through Clinging is conditioned the Becoming
Bhavapratyayā jāti yu yüan sheng

Through becoming is conditioned birth
Jātipratyayṃ jarāmaraṇam sheng yüan lao szu

Through Birth is conditioned old age, and death etc.

Six Kāma Heavens

1. *Caturmahārājā Tse ta wang ch'ung t'ien*

   The abodes of the four guardian kings of the four quarters, i.e. *Dhṛtarāṣtra* of the east, *Virūḍhaka* of the south, *Virūpākṣa* of the West, and *Vaiśravaṇa* of the north.

2. *Trayastriṃśa San shih san t'ien*

   Heaven of the thirty-three gods, i.e., eight *vāsavas*, two *Aśvins*, eleven *Rudras*, and Twelve *Ādityas.*

3. *Yāma Ye mo t'ien*

   The adode of the gods called *Yāmas*

4. *Tuṣita Tu shih t'ien*
   The abode of the gods who pass their days with pleasure only.

5. *Nirmāṇarati Lo pien hua t'ien*

   The heaven where the subjective desires are at once transformed into objective pleasure.

6. *Paranirmitavaśavartī Ta hua tzu tsai t'ien*
   The abode where the gods enjoy the pleasures earned by others.

Seventeen Rūpa Heavens

1. *Brahmakāyika Fan ch'ung t'ien*
   The Heaven of *Brahma's* retainers

2. *Brahmapurohita Fan fu t'ien*
   The Heaven of *Brahma's* ministers.

3. *Mahābrahman Ta fan t'ien* 大梵天
The Heaven of *Brahma* himself

4. *Parittābhā Shao kuang t'ien* 少光天
The Heaven of lesser light

5. *Apramāṇābha Wu liang kuang t'ien* 無量光天
The Heaven of infinite light

6. *Ābhāsvara chi kuang ching t'ien* 極光淨天
The Heaven of universal light

7. *Parīttaśubha Shao ching t'ien* 少淨天
The Heaven of lesser purity

8. *Apramāṇaśubha Wu liang ching t'ien* 無量淨天
The Heaven of infinite purity

9. *Śubhakṛtsna Pien ching t'ien* 遍淨天
The Heaven of universal purity

10. *Anabhraka Wu yün t'ien* 無雲天
The cloudless Heaven

11. *Puṇyaprasava Fu sheng t'ien* 福生天
The Heaven of fortunate birth

12. *Bṛhatphala K'uang kuo t'ien* 廣果天
The Heaven of great result

13. *Avrha Wu fan t'ien* 無煩天
The passionless Heaven

14. *Atapa Wu je t'ien* 無熱天
The Heaven without heat

15. *Sudṛśa Shan hsien t'ien* 善現天
The Heaven of perfect form

善見天

16. *Sudarśana Shan chien t'ien*
The Heaven of perfect vision

17. *Akaniṣṭha Se chiu ching t'ien*
The highest Heaven

CLASSIFICATION OF ELEMENTS IN THE *A-P'I-TA-MO-P'IN-LEI-TSU-LUN* *ABHIDHARMA-PRAKARAṆA-PĀDA-SĀSTRA*

1. Classification of Five *Dharmas*[1]

A. Listing of Items of five dharmas

The five *dharmas* are :

I.	*Rūpa*	(matter)
II.	*Citta*	(mind)
III.	*Caitta*	(mental attributes)
IV.	*Cittaviprayukta saṃskāra*	(*dharmas* not associated with mind)
V.	*Asaṃskṛta*	(Non-created).

I. *Rūpa* is defined as those which have *rūpa*, i.e., the four *mahābhūtas* (great elements, *ta chung*) and those which are composed of *rūpa*,[2] i.e., the five sense organs and their objects. The four are :

1.	*Prithvīdhātu*	Elements of Earth
2.	*Āpodhātu*	Elements of Water
3.	*Tejodhātu*	Elements of Fire
4.	*Vāyudhātu*	Elements of Air

The five sense organs are :

1.	*Cakṣurindriya*	Faculty of Eye
2.	*Śrotrendriya*	Faculty of Ear
3.	*Ghrāṇendriya*	Faculty of Nose
4.	*Jihvendriya*	Faculty of Tongue
5.	*Kāyendriya*	Faculty of Body

The five sense objects are :

1.	*Rūpa*	Form
2.	*Śabda*	Sound
3.	*Gandha*	Smell
4.	*Rasa*	Taste
5.	*Sparśa*	Touch

II. *Citta* is defined as *yi shih* (*manovijñāna*) which is the six *vijñānakāyas* (group of consciousness)[3], i.e.,

1.	*Cakṣurvijñāna*	Eye consciousness
2.	*Śrotravijñāna*	Ear consciousness
3.	*Ghrāṇavijñāna*	Smell consciousness
4.	*Jihvāvijñāna*	Eye consciousness
5.	*Kāyavijñāna*	Body consciousness
6.	*Manovijñāna*	Mind consciousness

III. *Caitta* refers to the *dharmas* associated with the mind (*cittasamprayukta, hsin suo fa*). They are :

1.	*Vedanā*	Feeling
2.	*Saṃjñā*	Notion
3.	*Cetanā*	Volition

4.	*Sparśa*	Contact
5.	*Manasikāra*	Attention
6.	*Chanda*	Desire
7.	*Adhimukti*	Approbation
8.	*Smṛti*	Memory
9.	*Samādhi*	Concentration
10.	*Prajñā*	Discernment
11.	*Śraddhā*	Faith
12.	*Vīrya*	Energy
13.	*Vitarka*	Intellectual reflection
14.	*Vicāra*	Investigation
15.	*Pramāda*	Carelessness
16.	*Apramāda*	Vigilance
17.	*Kuśalamūlas*	Good Roots
18.	*Akuśalamūlas*	Bad Roots
19.	*Avyākṛtamūlas*	Indeterminate Roots
20.	*Saṃyojanas*	Connections
21.	*Bandha*	Bond
22.	*Anuśayas*	Latent tendencies
23.	*Upakleśas*	Secondary Defilements
24.	*Paryavasthānas*	Wrappings of Attachment
25.	*Jñāna*	Knowledge

26. *Dṛṣṭi*	Views
27. *Abhisamaya*	Realisation

Furthermore, all *dharmas* of this type (*lei*) associated with the mind are *caitta*.[4]

IV. *Cittaviprayuktasaṃskāra* refers to the *dharmas* not associated with the mind. They are :

1. *Prāpti*	Acquisition
2. *Asaṃjñisamāpatti*	Absorption of Unconsciousness
3. *Nirodhasamāpatti*	Absorption of Extinction
4. *Āsaṃjñika*	Unconsciousness
5. *Jivītendriya*	Vital Organ
6. *Nikāyasabhāgatā*	Commonness of nature
7. *Āśrayaprāpti*	Acquisition of support
8. *Dravyaprāpti*	Acquisition of substance
9. *Āyatanaprāpti*	Acquisition of base
10. *Jāti*	Birth
11. *Jarā*	Decay
12. *Sthiti*	Subsistence
13. *Anityatā*	Impermanence
14. *Nāmakāya*	Names for signifying a person or object
15. *Padakāya*	Sentences

16.	*Vyañjanakāya*	Letters

All *dharmas* of the type which are not associated with the mind are *cittaviprayuktasaṃskāra*.[5]

V. *Asaṃskṛta* is threefold :[6]

1.	*Ākāśa*	Space
2.	*Apratisaṃ-khyānirodha*	Extinction that is not disjunction
3.	*Pratisaṃ-khyānirodha*	Extinction that is disjunction

B. Analysis of the items on five dharmas

I. Analysis of *rūpa* - The characteristics of the four *mahābhūtas* are mentioned as the following. The characteristics of *pṛthvīdhātu* is *kharatva* (hardness); of *āpodhātu* is *snehatva* (humidity); of *tejodhātu* is *uṣṇatva* (heat); of *vāyudhātu* is *īraṇa* (moton).[7]

Each of the five sense organs are defined as the subtle *rūpa* that is the support (*āśraya*) of each of the five consciousnesses respectively. For example,

'What is *cakṣurindriya*? It is the subtle *rūpa* that is the support of eye consciousness or *cakṣurvijñāna*.[8] Other sense organs are defined in the same way.

The characteristics and classification of the five objects are as the following :

Rūpa is that which has form. Some forms are well manifested (*hao hsing, vijñapti*) while some are' badly' manifested (*e hsing*), and some are between the two, like the manifested *rūpāyatana*.

Śabda is two fold - (1) that which is produced by the *mahābhūtas* having the power of sensation (*upāttamahābhūta*?)

and (2) that which is produced by the *mahābhūtas* not having the power of sensation (*anupāttamahābhūta*?).

Gandha is threefold- good (*hao*), bad (*e*), and equal *samagandha).*

Rasa is fourfold - (1) that which 'suits one's idea' (*k'e yi*); (2) that which does not' suit one's idea (*pu k'e yi*) (3) favourable (*shun*); and (4) indifferent(*she*).

Sparśa has seven characteristics : smoothness, roughness, lightness, heaviness, cold, hunger, and thirst.

Avijñapti rūpa (wu piao se) is defined as ' *rūpa* that is received by *dharmāyatana.*

II. Analysis of *citta* (the six *vijñānakāyas*) - six *vijñānakāyas* are defined in the following way ;

Cakṣurvijñāna is every perception (*liao pieh*) of *rūpa* on the support of *caksurindriya.*

Śrotravijñāna is every perception of *śabda* on the support of *śrotrendriya.*

In this way other *vijñānakāyas* are explained.[9]

III. Analysis of *caitta*- the characteristics and classification of *caitta* are as the following :[10]

1. *Vedanā* is of the nature of *anubhava* (experience). It is threefold ;

1. *Sukhavedanā*	Feeling of pleasure
2. *Duḥkhavedanā*	Feeling of pain
3. *Aduḥkhasukha-vedanā*	Feeling of neither pleasure nor pain

2. *Saṃjñā* has the nature of *viṣayanimittodgrāha* (determining characteristics of an object). It is threefold ;

1. *Parīttasaṃjñā* ?	Notion of small

2. *Mahāsaṃjñā*?	Notion of big
3. *Apramāṇa saṃjñā?*	Notion of immeasurable

3. *Cetana* is *cittābhisaṃskāra* or *manaskarma* (conditioning of the mind to create). It is threefold :

1. *Kuśalacetanā*	Volition of good
2. *Akuśalacetanā*	Volition of bad
3. *Avyākṛtacetanā*	Volition of indeterminate

4. *Sparśa* is the conjoinment of the three (*tṛkasannipāta*), i.e., the organ, the object and the consciousness.

5. *Manasikāra* is modification of the mind (*cetasa ābhogaḥ*). It is threefold :

1. *śaikṣa manasikāra*	Attention of Noble Learner
2. *Aśaikṣa manasikāra*	Attention of Non-learner
3. *Naśaikṣa nāśaikṣa manasikāra*	Attention of neither a noble learner nor Non-learner

6. *Chanda* is desire for action (*kartṛkāmyatā*).

7. *Adhimukti* is a certain state of mind of approbation, of the nature of approbation in the past and in the future.

8. *Smṛti* is clear recollection (*abhilapanatā*) by the mind.

9. *Samādhi* is the unity of the mind with the object *(cittaikāgratā*).

10. *Prajñā* is discernment of *dharmas.*

11. *Sraddhā* is classification of the mind.

12. *Vīrya* is endurance of the mind.

13. *Vitarka* is investigation by the mind in a crude manner.

14. *Vicāra* is investigation by the mind in a subtle manner.

15. *Pramāda* is non-cultivation of good *dharmas.*

16. *Apramāda* is cultivation of good *dharmas.*

17. *Kuśalamūla* is threefold :

1. *Alobha*	Non-greed
2. *Adveṣa*	Non-anger
3. *Amoha*	Non-delusion

18. *Akuśalamūla* is threefold :

1. *Lobha*	Greed
2. *Dveṣa*	Anger
3. *Moha*	Delusion

19. *Avyākṛtamūla* is fourfold :

1.*Avyākṛtatṛṣṇā*	Indeterminate craving
2. *Avyākṛtadṛṣṭi*	Indeterminate view
3. *Avyākṛtamāna*	Indeterminate pride
4.*Avyākṛta avidyā*	Indeterminate ignorance

20. *Saṃyojana* is nine fold :

1. *Tṛṣṇā*	Connection of craving
2. *Vyāpāda*	Connection of ill-will
3. *Māna*	Connection of pride
4. *Avidyā*	Connection of ignorance

5. *Dṛṣṭi*	Connection of view
6. *Parāmarśa*	Connection of attachment
7. *Vicikitsā*	Connection of doubt
8. *Īrṣyā*	Connection of envy
9. *Mātsarya*	Connection of parsimony

Tṛṣṇā is defined as lust (*rāga*) of *kāmadhātu, rūpadhātu* and *ārūpyadhātu.*

Vyāpāda is that which causes injury to others.

The classsification and characeristics of *māna* are as the following :

Māna is to elevate oneself in relation to others.

Atimāna is a state of excessive conceit.

Mānātimāna is a state of inordinate conceit.

Asmimāna is a state of self-conceit.

ūnamāna is a state of self-disrespect conceit.

Mithyāmāna is a state of false conceit.

Avidyā is ignorance of the three *dhātus.*

Dṛṣṭi is threefold ;

1. *Satkāyadṛṣṭi* - 'Personality view' which is to belief in a self and in things pertaining to self (*ātmātmīyagrāha*) with regard to the five *upādānaskandhas* (*satkāya*) or to take the latter as 'I' and 'mine'.[11]

2. *Antagrāhadṛṣṭi* -' View in extremes' which is to belief in the eternity or in annihilation of what one believes to be a self.[12]

3. *Mithyādṛṣṭi* -'False view' which is the view that negates (*pang*) cause, fruit, action or realities. [13]

Parāmarśa is two fold :

1. *Dṛṣṭiparāmarśa* - 'Attachment to a particular view' is to consider the five *upādānaskandhas* as excellent and the highest so as to produce *kṣayajñāna, sukha* and *prajñā* for the 'seeing (*darśana*).[14]

2. *Śīlavrataparāmarśa* - 'Attachment to mere rules and rituals' is to consider the five *upādānaskandhas* as capable of producing purity or *nirvāṇa*, from which arises *kṣayajñāna* etc.[15]

Vicikitsā - It is uncertainty of the mind with reference to truth.[16]

Īrṣyā is to wish for own reputation.

Mātsarya is attachment to wealth.

21. *Bandha* refers to all the *anuśayas.* It is threefold :

1. *Rāga*	Lust
2. *Lobha*	Greed
3. *Moha*	Delusion

22. *Anuśaya*- It is sevenfold:[17]

1. *Kāmarāga*	Lust of desire
2. *Pratigha*	Anger
3. *Sarāga*	Attached with lust
4. *Māna*	Pride
5. *Avidyā*	Ignorance
6. *Dṛṣṭi*	View
7. *Vicikitsā*	Doubt

kāmarāgānuśaya is five fold :

1. *Rāga* concerned with the *kāmadhātu* that is to be

abandoned by the Seeing of suffering.

2. *Rāga*........Seeing of Origin

3. *Rāga*........Seeing of Extinction

4. *Rāga*.......Seeing of the Path

5. *Rāga*........by Meditation

Pratighānuśaya is fivefold :

1. *Pratigha* to be abandoned by the Seeing of suffering.

2. *Pratigha*.........Seeing of Origin

3. *Pratigha*.......Seeing of Extinction

4. *Pratigha*.......Seeing of the Path

5. *Pratigha*........by Meditation

Sarāgānuśaya is tenfold:

1. *Sarāga* concerned with the *rūpadhātu* that is to be abandoned by the Seeing of suffering

2. *Sarāga*........Seeing of Origin

3. *Sarāga*.......Seeing of Extinction

3. *Sarāga*........Seeing of the Path

5. *Sarāga*......By Meditation

6. *Sarāga* concerned with the *ārūpyadhātu*........Seeing of suffering.

7. *Sarāga*.........Seeing of Origin

8. *Sarāga*........Seeing of Extinction

9. *Sarāga*........Seeing of the Path

10. *Sarāga*........By Meditation

Mānānuśaya is fifteen in number.

1. *Māna* concerned with *rūpadhātu* that is to be abandoned by the Seeing of suffering.
2. *Māna*.......Seeing of Origin
3. *Māna*.......Seeing of Extinction
4. *Māna*......Seeing of the Path
5. *Māna*.....By Meditation
6. *Māna* concerned with the *rūpadhātu* that is to be abandoned by the Seeing of Suffering
7. *Māna*........Seeing of Origin
8. *Māna*.......Seeing of Extinction
9. *Māna*........Seeing of the Path
10. *Māna*........By Meditation
11. *Māna* concerned with the *Ārūpyadhātu* that is to be abandoned by the Seeing of Suffering
12. *Māna*.........Seeing of Origin
13. *Māna*.........Seeing of Extinction
14. *Māna*.......Seeing of the Path
15. *Māna*.......By Meditation

Avidyānuśaya is fifteen in number :

1. *Avidyā* concerned with the *kāmadhātu* that is to be abandoned by the Seeing of Suffering
2. *Avidyā*..........Seeing of Origin
3. *Avidyā*........Seeing of Extinction
4. *Avidyā*......Seeing of the Path
5. *Avidyā*........By Meditation
6. *Avidyā* concerned with the *rūpadhātu* that is to be

abandoned by the Seeing of Suffering

7. *Avidyā*..........Seeing of Origin

8. *Avidyā*..........Seeing of Extinction

9. *Avidyā*........Seeing of the Path

10. *Avidyā*........By Meditation.

11. *Avidyā* concerned with the *ārūpya* that is to be abandoned by the Seeing of Suffering

12. *Avidyā*......Seeing of Origin

13. *Avidyā*........Seeing of Extinction

14. *Avidyā*..........Seeing of Path

15. *Avidyā*..........By Meditation

Dṛṣṭyānuśaya is thirty-six in number.

A.12 Concerned with the *kāmadhātu*

B.12 Concerned with the *rūpadhātu*

C.12 Concerned with *ārūpyadhātu.*

A. 1. *Satkāyadṛṣṭi* concerned with the *kāmadhātu* that is to abandoned by the Seeing of Suffering

2. *Satkāyadṛṣṭi*...........Seeing of the Path

3. *Antagrāhadṛṣṭi*.........Seeing of Suffering

4. *Antagrāhadṛṣṭi*.........Seeing of the Path

5. *Mithyādṛṣti*..........Seeing of Origin

6. *Mithyādṛṣṭi*.........Seeing of Extinction

7. *Mithyādṛṣṭi*.......Seeing of the Path

8. *Dṛṣṭiparāmarśa*........Seeing of Origin

9. *Dṛṣṭiparānarśa*......Seeing of Extinction

10. *Dṛṣṭiparāmarśa*..........Seeing of the Path

11. *Sīlavrataparāmarśa*........Seeing of Origin

12. *Sīlavrataparāmarśa*..:.........Seeing of Extinction

In this way B.12 and C.12 are to be explained. *Vicikitsānuśaya* is twelve in number.

1. *Vicikitsā* concerned with the *kāmadhātu* that is to be abandoned by the Seeing of Suffering

2. *Vicikitsā*........Seeing of Origin

3. *Vicikitsā*........Seeing of Extinction

4. *Vicikitsā*.......Seeing of the Path

5. *Vicikitsā* concerned with the *rūpadhātu*...........Seeing of suffering

6. *Vicikitsā*...........Seeing of Origin

7. *Vicikitsā*..........Seeing of Extinction

8. *Vicikitsā*...........Seeing of the Path

9. *Vicikitsā*. concerned with the *ārūpyadhātu*.........Seeing of suffering

10. *Vicikitsā*..........Seeing of Origin

11. *Vicikitsā*.........Seeing of Extinction

12. *Vicikitsā*..........Seeing of the path

23. *Upakleśas* - All the *anuśayas* are *upakleśas* but all the *upakelśas* are not *anuśayas.*

24. *Paryavasthānas* are eightfold :

1. *Styāna* Torpidmindedness

2. *Auddhatya* Dissipation

3. *Middha* Drowsiness

4. *Kaukṛtya* Remorse

5. *Īrṣyā* Envy

6. *Mātsarya* Parsimony

7. *Āhrīkya* Absence of sense of shame

8. *Anapatrāpya* Absence of fear of blame

25. *jñāna* - It is tenfold :

1. *Dharmajñāna* (knowledge of *dharma*) is a pure knowledge concerned with the *kāmadhātu*, of the four Noble Truths.[18]

2. *Anvayajñāna* (Inferential knowledge) is a pure knowledge concerned with the *rūpadhátu* and the *ārūpyadhātu*, of the four Noble Truths.[19]

3. *Paracittajñāna* (knowledge of the mind of others) is that which is obtained by meditation of the mind and mental states of others.[20]

4. *Lokasaṃvṛtijñāna* (Conventional knowledge) is a defiled discernment (*sāsrava prajñā*).[21]

5. *Duḥkhajñāna* (Knowledge about suffering) is a knowledge of impermanence, miserableness, and egolessness of the five *skandhas*.[22]

6. *Samudayajñāna* (Knowledge of Origin) is a pure knowledge about the fact that the impure (*sāsrava*) is conditioned by the relation of the cause and the effect.[23]

7. *Nirodhajñāna* (Knowledge of Extinction) is a pure knowledge about extinction, proper (*samyak*), calm (*śānta*), excellent (*praṇīta*) and liberation.[24]

8. *Mārgajñāna* (Knowledge of the Path) is a pure knowledge about the fact that the Noble (eight fold) path of

proper understanding leads to liberation (*ru hsing chu*).[25]

9. *Kṣayajñāna* (Knowledge of Destruction) is a pure knowledge about the four stages in the realisation of the four Noble Truths.[26]

10. *Anutpādajñāna* (Knowledge of Non-arising) is a pure knowledge subsequent to the realisation of the four Noble Truths (*Satyābhisamaya*).[27]

IV. Analysis of *Cittaviprayukta Saṃskāra.*

1. *Prāpti* is defined as the acquisition of all the *dharmas.*

2. *Asaṃjñāisamāpatti*- it is cessation of the mind and mental states having for its antecedent the idea of departure attached to the abandoning of the defilement of the *Śubhakarakṛtsna* but not to the abandoning of higher defilements.[28]

3. *Nirodhasamāpatti* is the cessation of the mind and the mental states having for its antecedent the idea of calm attached to the abandoning of the defilement of *ākiṃcanyāyatana.*[29]

4. *Āsaṃjñika* is the cessation of the mind and the mental states of those who are born among the *Asaṃjñisattva* gods.[30]

5. *Jivītendriya* is the life (*āyus*) of the three *Dhātus.*[31]

6. *Nikāyasabhāgatā* is the commonness of nature (*tung lei hsing*).[32]

7. *Āśrayaprāpti* is the acquisition of the support base(*āśrayāyatana*).

8. *Dravyaprāpti* is the acquisition of the groups of existence (*skandhas*)

9. *Āyatanaprāpti* is the acquisition of the internal and the external bases.

10. *Jāti* is the life arising from the *Skandhas.*

11. *Jarā* is maturation of the *Skandhas.*

12. *Sthiti* is the non-perishing of the *saṃskāras* which have formerly arisen in the life.[35]

13 *Anityatā* is the destruction of the *saṃskāras* which have formely arisen in life.[36]

14. *Nāmakāya* is' word that adds or increases' (*tseng yu*).[37]

15. *Padakāya* is ' complete sentence.'[38]

16. *Vyāñjanakāya* is' multitude of letters.[39]

V. Analysis of *Asaṃskṛta*

1. *Ākāśa* is that' which does not hinder *rūpa* as *rūpa* takes place freely in the *ākāṣa.*[40]

2. *Apratisaṃkhyānirodha* is an extinction which is different from disjunction (*visaṃyoga*).[41]

3. *Pratisaṃkhyānirodha* is disjunction.[42]

2. Classification of knowledges

The definitions of the ten knowledges are already given in the previous section. The following classification of the ten knowledges are now to be discussed :

A. What are the objects (*ālambana, suo yuan*)?

B. How ten knowledges are included in another?

C. How many of the ten knowledges are pure, how many impure?

D. How many of ten knowledges are conditioned by the created, how many by the non-created?

A. *Dharmajñāna* has its object all the *saṃskāras* concerned with the *kāmadhātu* and one part of pure *anāsrava dharma*, because it realises the *samskāras* concerned with the *kāmadhātu,* their origin, and extinction along with the path by which those *saṃskāras* are to be abandoned.

Anvayajñāna has its object all the *saṃskāras* concerned with the *rūpadhātu* and the *ārūpyadhātu* and one part of pure *dharma,* because it realises the *saṃskāras* concerned with the *rūpadhātu* and the *ārūpyadhātu*, their origin and extinction along with the path by which these *saṃskāras* are to be abandoned.

Paracittajñāna has its object the mind, the mental states of others concerned with the *kāmadhātu* and the *rūpadhātu* appearing together in the present, and a part of pure mind and mental states of others; becuase *paracittajñāna* realises the same.

Lokasaṃvṛtijñāna has its object all the *dharmas* as it realises that which leads to truth, or that which leads to no-truth, or that which leads to neither truth nor no-truth.

Duḥkhajñāna has its object the five *upādanaskandhas* as it realises the impermanence, miserableness, voidness and selflessness of them.

Samudayajñāna bears on the cause of impure *dharmas* as it realises that the impure *dharmas* are conditioned by the relation of cause and effect.

Nirodhajñāna bears on the proper extinction as it realises extinction as proper, calm, excellent and liberation.

Mārgajñāna bears on the *śaikṣa* and the *aśaikṣa dharmas*,i.e., the eightfold path leads to liberation.

Kṣayajñāna bears on all conditioned *dharmas* and proper extinction as by it one himself realises that 'Suffering is completely known to me, its Origin is abandoned by me, its Extinction has been actualised by me, the Path has been cultivated by me.'

Anutpādajñāna bears on all conditoned *dharmas* and proper extinction, as by it one himself realises that' Suffering is completely known to me and it no longer to be known........ the Path is no longer to be cultivated.[43]

B. Among ten knowledges, *dharmajñāna* is made up of one full knowledge and one part of seven other knowledges,i.e., the *kāmadhātu* part of the knowledge of Suffering, of Origin, of Extinction, of the Path, the knowledge of other mind, the knowledge of Destruction, the knowledge of Non-arising.

Inferential knowledge is made up of one full knowledge and one part of seven other knowledges, i.e., the part concerned with the *rūpadhātu* and the *ārupyadhātu* of the knowledge of Suffering, of Origin, of Extinction, of the Path, the Knowledge of other mind, the Knowledge of Destruction, and the Knowledge of Non-arising.

The knowledge of the mind of other is made up of one full knowledge and one part of four knowledges of *dharmas*, Inferential knowledge, knowledge of the Path, and Conventional knowledge.

Conventional knowledge is made up of one full knowledge and one part of another knowledge,i.e., the impure (*yu pien*) part of the mind of other.

The knowledge of Suffering is made up of one full knowledge and one part of four other knowledges,i.e., the knowledge of *dharmas*, inferential knowledge, the knowledge of Destruction, and the knowledge of Non-arising.

The knowledge of Origin and Extinction are explained in the same manner.

A knowledge of the Path is made up of one full knowledge and one part of the five knowledges, i.e., the knowledge of the *dharmas*, Inferential knowledge, the knowledge of Destruction, the knowledge of non-arising, and the knowledge of the mind of other.

The knowledge of Destruction is made up of one full knowledge and one part of six knowledges,i.e., the knowledge of *dharmas*, Inferential knowledge, the knowledge of Suffering, of Origin, of Extinction, and of the Path.[44]

C. Among the ten knowledge, one is pure, eight are impure, and one is to be discriminated, like *paracittajñāna* which is either impure (when it realises the impure mind and the mental states of the others) or pure (when it realises the pure mind and the mental states of the others).[45]

Among the ten knowledges, *Duḥkhajñāna* and *Samudayajñāna* are conditioned by impure (i.e., suffering and its origin), *Nirodhajñāna* and *Margajñāna* are conditioned by pure (i.e., extinction and the path) while the other six knowledges are conditoned by either impure or pure *dharmas.*[46]

D. Among the ten knowledge, *Dharmajñāna, Anvayajñāna, kṣayajñāna, Anutpādajñāna* and *Lokasaṃ vṛtijñāna* are conditioned either by created or by non-created *dharmas.* The four knowledges of Suffering, of Origin, of the Path, and of the mind of the others are conditioned by the created *dharmas. Nirodhajñāna* is conditioned by the non-created *dharmas.*[47]

3. Classification of Bases

Twelve bases (*āyatana, chu*), i.e., six sense organs and six object of sense are classified in the following way.[48]

a) How many of the twelve bases are with *rūpa*, how many without *rūpa*?

b) How many of the.......with vision,.......without vision?

c) How many of the.......impure,........pure?

d) How many........are determinate,.......indeterminate?

e) How many.........to be meditated,.........not to be meditated?

f) How many......matured,..........not matured?

g) How many.........internal.........external?

h) How many..........grasped by feeling.......not grasped by feeling?

i) How many........with mind,.......without mind?

j) How many.......with mental states,........without mental states?

k) How many.........have objects,.......do not have objects?

l) How many.........with *karma*(action),.......without *karma*?

m) How many........good,....bad,.....indeterminate?

n) How many.......abandoned by Seeing,......abandoned by Meditation......not abandoned?

o) How many.........for Noble learner,.......for Non learner,....... for neither learner, nor Non-learner.

p) How many........concerned with the *kāmadhātu*,......with the *rūpadhātu*, ...with the *ārūpyadhātu*,.....not concerned with the *dhātus*?

q) How many......are past,.......future,.......presesnt?

r) How many.......are included in the Truth of Suffering,.....Origin.....Extinction......the Path?

s) How many......are to be abandoned by Seeing the Suffering?.......Origin?.......Extinction?........the Path?........Meditation ?

Besides, five groups(*skandha*) and eighteen Elements (*dhātu*) and their relation with the twelve bases are also discussed.

4. Classification of Mental States

In section 4 of the *APPS*, various mental states are enumerated as the following:[49]

a) Ten *mahābhūmika dharmas* that refer to the first ten *caittas* explained earlier in A.III (Analysis of *caitta*)

b) Ten *mahākuśalabhūmika dharmas,* i.e., *śraddhā* (Faith), *vīrya* (Energy), *hrī* (Shame), *apatrapā* (Fear of blame), *alobha* (Non-greed), *adveṣa* (Non-anger), *praśrabdhi* (Composure), *upekṣā* (Equanimity), *apramāda* (Vigilance), *ahiṃsā* (Non-injury).

c) Ten *mahākleśabhūmika dharmas*, i.e., *āśraddhya* (Unbelief), *kausīdya* (Indolence), *muṣitasmṛtitā* (Forgetfulness), *vikṣepa* (Distraction), *avidyā* (Ignorance), *asamprajānya* (Non-discernment), *ayoniśo manasikāra* (Wrong attention), *mithyādhimokṣa* (Wrong approbation), *auddhatya* (Dissipation) and *pramāda* (Carelessness)

d) Ten *parīttakleśamahābhūmika dharmas*, i.e., *krodha* (Fury), *upanāha* (Enmity), *mrakṣa* (Hypocricy), *pradāsa* (Vexation), *īrṣyā* (Envy), *mātsarya* (Parsimony), *sāṭhya* (Deception), *māya*(Duplicity), *mada*(Pride), *vihiṃsā* (Harmfulness)

e) The five *indriyas* (Faculties), *the* five *dharmas* (*vitarka, vicāra, vijñāna, āhrīkya*, and *anaptrāpya*), the six *saṃsparśakāyas*(Groups of Contact), the six *vedanākāyas* (Groups of Feeling), the six *saṃjñā-kāyas* (Groups of Notion), the six *cetanākāyas*(Groups of Volition) and the six *tṛṣṇākāyas.* These classifications have been detailed elsewhere.[50]

The nature of the ten *mahābhūmika* (Basic states) and the first two among the *mahākuśalabhūmika* (Pure states) has already been explained in the analysis of *caittas.* The special characteristics of the other states are now described.

Among the *mahābhūmika dharmas, hrī* is sense of shame, to regard or respect good *dharmas. Apatrapā* is sense of fear of blame at one's sins. *Alobha* is to remain detached from the existence and to counteract greed. *Adveṣa* is to remain unirritated and to counteract anger. *Praśrabdhi* is ease and composure. *Upekṣā* is the state of equanimity of the body and the mind. *Apramāda* is to arrest defiled *dharmas* and to cultivate good *dharmas. Ahiṃsā* is not causing injury to the sentient beings.

Among the ten *mahākleśabhūmika, āśradhya* is contamination of the mind. *Kausīdya* is lalziness of minds in the cultivation of good *dharmas,* and cultivation of bad *dharmas. Muṣita smṛtitā* is not to remember objects clearly. *Vikṣepa* is lack of concentration of mind. *Avidyā* is ignorance of the three spheres of existence. The nature of *asaṃprajanya* is inexact idea that counteracts right understanding. *Ayoniśo manasikāra* is defiled attention. *Auddhatya* by nature is the state of mind not peaceful and tranquil. *Pramāda* is non-cultivation of the abandonment of bad *dharmas* and collection of good *dharmas.*

Among the ten *parīttakleśamahābhumikas, krodha* is every state of fury in the past, present and future. *Upanāha* is enduring enmity of the mind. *Mrakṣa* has the characteristics of hiding one's offence. The nature of *pradāsa* is the state of being very angry. *Īrṣyā* is the state of jealousy of others. The nature of *mātsarya* is miserly meanness. *Śāthya* is deceiving and misleading others. The states of deceitful mind is *māya. Mada* is the state of proud exaltation. Hurting the sentient beings along with the infliction of misery to them is the nature of *vihiṃsā.*

5. Classification of Latent Tendencies

The latent tendencies (*anuśaya*) are seven by nature (details in *A.* 111.22). The number of the *anuśayas* as ninety eight is obtained with reference to the three spheres (the *kāmadhātu, rūpadhātu* and the *ārūpyadhātu*) to which they belong and their mode of abandoning (seeing each of the four Truths and Meditation). This has already been discussed.

The *APPS* presents the classification of the *anuśayas* as the following:[51]

a) How many of the ninety eight *anuśayas* belong to the *kāmadhātu....* to the *rūpadhātu,*and to the *ārūpyadhātu* ? The answer is, thirty six in the *kāmadhātu,* thirty one in the *rūpadhātu* and thrity one in the *ārūpyadhātu.*

b) How many of the *anuśayas* of the *kāmadhātu* are abandoned by Seeing?.... How many by Meditation?

c) The meaning of the word *anuśāya* : It signifies *anuśayana(sui tseng), anuṣanga (sui chu), anubandha* (*sui fu*). The *anuśaya* which is not abandoned, not perfectly known' becomes active and grows' (*sui tseng*) by reason of its object and the *dharmas* associated with it, in the sphere (*dhātu)* to which it belongs.[52]

d) There are twelve *anuśayas* - *Kāmarāgānuśaya, Pratigha, Rūparāga, Ārūpyarāga, Māna, Avidyā, Satkāyadṛṣṭi, Antagrāhadṛṣṭi, Mithyādṛṣṭi, Dṛṣṭiparāmarśa, Śīlavrataparāmarśa, Vicikitsā nuśaya.*

e) How does *Kāmarāganuśaya* 'become active'? Because of the agreeable of the pleasant......... How so *pratigha?* Because of the disagreeable........How so *rūparāga?* Because of the agreeable...... why is *kāmarāganuśaya* produced? For three reasons: 1. *Kāmarāgānuśaya* is not abanodoned or completely known; 2. Some *dharmas* favourable to ' Wrappings of attachments' of the *Kāmarāga* present themselves, and 3. there is Wrong judgement (*ayoniśo manasikāra*)

These twelve *anuśayas* make seven by counting *rūparāga* and under the name of *bhavarāga;* by counting the five *dṛṣṭs* under *dṛṣṭyānuśaya.*

f) How many of the ninety eight are universal (*sarvatraga*), how many are non-universal?) Twenty seven are universal, sixty five are non-universal; and six are both.......)

g) How many of the ninety eight have impure *dharmas* as their object?

h) How many of the ninety eight have conditioned things for their object?

i) How many of the ninety eight become active and grow from their objects?..........from associated *dharmas*?........their objects and from associated *dharmas?*..........from neither the one or the other.

j) How many 'become active and grow' from the the *dharmas* abandoned by the Seeing of Suffering?.........from thoughts abandoned by the Seeing of Suffering?.......... from thoughts associated with a false view abandoned by the Seeing of Extinction?.........from an *avidyā* abandoned by the Seeing of Extincion?........ from an *avidyā* with a false view abandoned by the Seeing of Extinction?........etc.

6. Classification of *Dharma* in Numerical Order

1. One *dharma- jñeyadharma* (*dharma* to be known); *vijñeyadharma* (*dharma* to be cognized); *anumeyadharma* (*dharma* to be inferred) etc.[53]

2. Two *dharmas-rūpidharma* (*dharma* with *rupa),* *arūpidharma* (*dharma* without *rupa*) ; *sanidarśana* (one

'base', *āyatana*, *rūpāyatana*), *anidarśana* (eleven *āyatana*); capable of being struck (*sapratigha),* not capable of being struck (*apratigha)* etc. [54]

3. Three *dharmas-kuśala*(good), *akuśala* (bad), *avyākṛta* (indererminate) ; *śaikṣa* (learner), *aśaikṣa*(non-learner), *na śaikṣa* (neither learner nor non-learner) etc. [55]

4. Four *dharmas-*Four *smṛtyupasthānas,* i.e., application of mindfulness with regard to body (*kāya*), feeling (*vedanā*), mind*(citta)* and *dharmas;* Four *abhijñāpratipad,* i.e., progress to deliverance or four modes of progress: painful with slow comprehension, painful progress with quick comprehension, pleasant progress with quick comprehension etc. ; four noble truths; Four *śrāmaṇyaphala* (fruits of religious life) etc.[56]

Five *dharmas* - Five *upādānaskandhas* (five groups of clinging) i.e. *rūpaskandha, vedanāskandha, saṃjñāskandha, saṃkāraskandha,* and *vijñānaskandha*; Five *dharmas,* i.e. *rūpa, citta, caitta, cittaviprayukta saṃskāra* and *asaṃskṛta.*[57]

Six *dharmas*-Six elements, i.e., earth, water, fire, air, space and consciousness.[58]

Seven *dharmas* - Seven latent tendencies or *anuśayas*; seven *bodhygaṅgas* (factors of enlightenment) etc.

Eight *dharmas* - Eight *vimokṣas*[59] (deliverances), i.e., (i) *rūpi rūpāṇi paśyati* - when remaining in the sphere of *rūpa,* one perceives *rūpa,* (ii) *adhyātmam arūpasaṃjñi bahirdhā rūpāṇi paśyati* - without having the notion of internal forms, one perceives the external forms; (iii) *śubham vimokṣam kāyena sākṣātkṛtvopasampadya viharati* - realising himself the agreeable *vimokṣa,* he remains in the contemplation; (iv-vii) four *ārupya dhyanas*; (viii) the *saṃjñāvedita-nirodha-samāpatti.* These are the the eight *vimokṣas.*

Also, the Eightfold Path etc.

Nine *dharmas*- Nine *bandhas* etc.

Ten *dharmas* -Ten *kṛtsnāyatanas*[60] (All-encompassing bases) i.e., the totality of earth, water, fire, and wind; blue, yellow, red and white; and the uninterrupted bases (*ānantyāyatanas*) of space and consciousness (the First and the Second Absorptions of the *Ārūpyadhātu*). They are called `all encompassing' (*kṛtsna*) because they embrace their objects in their totality.

Eleven *dharmas* - defiled *rūpa* undefiled *rūpa*, defiled feeling - undefiled feeling, defiled *saṃjñā* - undefiled *saṃjñā*, defiled *saṃskāra* - undefiled *saṃskāra*, defiled *vijñāna* - undefiled *vijñāna*, defiled *asaṃskṛta* etc.

Twelve *dharmas* - Twelve bases etc.

Eighteen *dharmas* - Eighteen elements etc.

Twenty two Faculties (*indriya*) etc.

Ninety eight *anuśayas* etc. are defined separately in the *APPS*, p. 713 c20.

7. Classification on Buddhist Practices

One thousand questions on various ethical and meditational practices of Buddhism are discussed in the Seventh section of the *APPS.* Those are :

1. On Four *Sikṣāpadas* (Precepts), i.e. Abstaining from taking life, from what is not given, from unchastity, from lying and from the use of intoxicants (pp. 733a18-734c2)
2. On Four *Avetyaprasādas* (Attainments of faith and purity), i.e., Faith relating to the *aśaikṣa dharmas* of the Buddha, relating to the *Dharma* (four Noble Truths), relating to the *Saṅgha*, and relating to the

precepts dear to the saints or the four *aṅgas* of the learners (pp. 734c13-737-a2).

4. On Four *Abhijñāpratipadas* (Modes of progress) - See 6.4 for details (Chinese text in 737a2-738b14).

5. On Four *Āryavaṃsas* (Noble lineage), i.e., four classes of the Buddha's disciples who are content with clothing, with food, with bed and seat, and with the nature of taking delight of Extinction/Meditation (pp. 738b14-739b13).

6. On Four *Samyakpradhānas* (Right striving), i.e., Striving for the abandoning of bad states that have arisen, for the abandoning of bad states that have not arisen, for the arising of good states that have not arisen, and for the retaining of the good states that have arisen (*ibid*).

7. On Four *Ṛddhipādas* (Bases of power), i.e., concentration of Desire, of Energy, of the mind, and of Investigation (*Ibid*).

8. On Four *Smṛtyupasthānas* as mentioned in 6.4.

9. On Four *Āryasatyas* (Noble Truth), i.e., the truth of Suffering, of Arising of Extinction, of the Path (pp. 746a27-747b23).

10. On Four *Dhyānas* (Absorptions), i.e., the first, the second, the third and the fourth absorptions(pp.746a27-747b22).

11. On Four *Apramāṇas* (Immeasurables), i.e., having kindness (*maitrī*). Compassion (*karuṇā*), Sympathetic joy (*muditā*) and Equanimity (*upekṣā*). Details in pp. 747n23-748c11).

12. On Four *Ārūpyas* (Formless spheres), i.e., Sphere of Boundless space, of Boundless consciousness, of

Nothingness, of Neither-Notion-nor-absence of Notion (pp.748CR-750C21).

13. On Four cultivations of absorptions (*Bhāvanāsamādhi*),i.e., Absorption leading to attainment of happiness, of the Seeing of knowledge, of wisdom, and Absorption leading to the destruction of sensuous lust and attachments (pp.750C21-752C18).

14. On *Bodhyaṅga* (Seven Factors of enlightment), i.e., mindfulness, (*smṛti).* Truth investigation (*dharmavicaya*), Energy(*vīrya*), Rapture (*prīti*), Tranquility (*praśrabhi*), Concerntration (*samādhi*), and Equanimity (*upekṣā*). For details on questions see pp.752C19-753b8.

15 On Twenty-two *Indriyas* (Faculties)-for details on questions, see pp. 753b9-756C4.

16. On Twelve *Āyatanas* (Bases), Five *skandhas* (Groupings or Aggregates) and Eighteen *Dhātus* (Elements) - questions and answers on these are detailed in pp. 756C5-765C26.

Various questions and answers on the topics deal with (1) the different characteristics of the *dharmas* (like with or with ou t *rūpa;* visible, not visible; capable of being struck, not capable of being struck; conditioned, unconditioned, etc.),(2) modes of eradication of bad *dharmas* and (3) attainment of good *dharmas*. This has been demonstrated in the classification of Bases and Latent tendencies in Secton 3 and Section 5 respectively.

In Section 8 of the *APPS*, remarks are made on several points already discussed in the previous sections.

RÉSUMÉ

The contents of the eight sections of the *APPS* suggest classification or distinction of various physical and mental phenomena with regard to the theoretical and practical dimensions of the Buddha's teachings. The text makes a careful examination of the problems and suggestions introduced by the older method of classification as adopted in the original and early phases of *Abhidharma*, besides giving new classifications with elaborations and definitions. The first five sectionsof the text specially demonstrate the important aspects of this new development.

The five member classification of *dharmas* is a new scheme that examines all things objectively with detailed analysis of each member. The exposition of the ten forms of knowledge is an independent contribution to the development of the *Sarvāstivāda Abhidharma.* The classification of the *āyatanas* and the ninety eight *anuśayas* are also new additions. Elaboration of mental states and classification of *dharmas* in numerical order are characterized with the revisions and reclassifications of the earlier ones. Specially the classification of forty mental associates in tens is considered as a new explanation of the Buddhist psychology. The items treated in earlier *Abhidharma* treatise of the *Sarvāstivāda* are thus dealt in full and their deeper implications are considered on a rational basis.

Notes

1. Discussion on the topic is based on the Chinese text of the *APPS, T,* No.1542, Vol.26,pp.692b19-694b2.
2. *Ibid.*, p.692b20-22
3. *Ibid.*,p.692b23-25.
4. For details, see *ibid.*, p. 692b25-c5.
5. *Ibid.,* p. 692c5-8.
6. *Ibid.*, p. 692c8-10.
7. *Ibid.*, p. 692c11-12

8. *Ibid* .,p.692c12-13.

9. *Ibid.*, p. 693a5-9.

10. *Ibid.*, p. 693a10-21.

11 For details see, *AKB*, *op.cit.,* p. 772. Also see Pruden, *op.cit.,* vol. 3,pp.872-874.

12 *APPS, op,cit.,* p. 693b19-20.

13 *Ibid.*, p. 693b20-21.

14 cf, *AKB, op, cit.,* p. 773-*hīne agradrṣṭir drṣtiparāmarśah.*

15 *APPS,op,cit.,* p. 693b23-25.

16 *Ibid.,* p. 693b25-26.

17 For details on the *anuśayas* and their abandoning by seeing the four Truths or by Meditation, see *ibid.,* p. 693b28-c18.

18 *Ibid.*, p. 693c23-26.

19 *Ibid.*, p. 693c 26-28.

20 *Ibid.*, p. 693c29-694a2.

21 cf. *ibid.,* p. 694a3.

22 *Ibid.,* p. 694a3-4.

23 *Ibid.*, p. 694a4-6.

24 *Ibid.,* p. 694a6-7.

25 *Ibid.*, p. 694a7-8.

26 *Ibid.*, p. 694a8-10.

27 *Ibid.*, p. 694a10-14.

28 *Ibid.,* p. 694a19-20.

29 *Ibid.*, p. 694a20-22.

30 *Ibid.*, p. 694a22-23.

31 *Ibid.*

32 *Ibid.*, p. 694a23-24.

33 *Ibid.*, p. 694a25-26.

34 *Ibid.*, p. 694a26.

35 *Ibid.*, p. 694a26-27.

36 *Ibid.*, p. 694a27.

37 *Ibid.*, p. 694a28.

38 *Ibid.*

39 *Ibid.*, p. 694a29.

40 *Ibid.*, p. 694a29-b1.

41 *Ibid.*

42 *Ibid.*, p. 694b2.

43 The discussion on the objects of ten knowledges is based on the original *APPS* (in Chinese), *Ibid.*, p. 694b4-c4.

44 For details on the inclusion of the ten knowledges in another see *ibid.*, pp. 649c5-696a23.

45 *Ibid.*, p. 694a24-26.

46 *Ibid.*, p. 694a26-27.

47 *Ibid.*, p. 694b7-13.

48 The discussion is a summary of the questions on the classifications of the bases in the *APPS*, *ibid.*, pp. 696b15-698a27.

49 The mental states have been examined in the *APPS*,

pp. 698a28-701c29.

50 The *ADPS* has the same classification. See details in Swati Ganguly, *Treatise on Groups of Elements, op.cit.*, pp. 18-30.

51 The discussion is a summary of the classifications of the latent tendencies in the *APPS*, *ibid.*, pp. 702a8-711b5.

52 For details on this problem, see *ibid.*, pp. 702b22-711b5.

53 *Ibid.*, p. 711b7.

54 *Ibid.*, p. 711b8.

55 *Ibid.*, p. 711c26.

56 *Ibid.*, p. 711b23.

57 *Ibid.*, p. 711b25.

58 *Ibid.*, p. 711c2.

59 *Ibid.*, p. 711c20-29.

60.cf. *ibid.*, p. 713b21-27.

A-p'i-ta-mo-chieh-shen-tsu-lun, (tr.) Hsüan-tsang, A.D.

APPENDIX

INTRODUCTION OF *SARVĀSTIVĀDA ABHIDHARMA* IN CHINA : A STUDY ON SAṄGHADEVA

The doctrines of *Abhidharma* teachings were introduced in China in the last quarter of the fourth century A.D. by the great Indian teacher and scholar of the *Sarvāstivāda* tradition of Buddhism, Gautama Saṅghadeva[1] (Chutan Seng-Chieh-ti-p'o, arrived in China in A.D. 383) from Kashmir. Saṅghadeva implanted Buddhist philosophy in the soil of China by teaching and preaching the Kashmiri *Sarvāstivāda abhidharma* doctrines at various Buddhist centres in China. Moreover, he trained Chinese monks in translation works in the formative phase of the translations of the Buddhist texts in China. Above all, original *Sarvāstivāda* texts are preserved only in Chinese translations done by him. In this paper we will try to examine the different phases of Saṅghadeva's missionary activities in China. The focus primarily will be on his contribution to the promotion of the *Sarvāstivada abhidharma* learning. The challanges he and the other Buddhists faced in propagating Buddhist doctrines in the fourth century China, however, will be analysed occassionally. In the beginning, a brief discussion on the *Sarvastivada abhidharma* is presented.

I

The *Sarvastivada abhidharma* had a long history in Kashmir before it was transmitted to China through Central

Asia. *Abhidharma* means "discourse or study on the *dharma*".[2] It is a class of literature that deals with the analytical and theological aspects of the Buddha's teachings. The *Abhidharma* developed along with the emergency of different sects of Buddhism in India.[3] The most important sect of the *Hīnayāna* was the *Sarvāstivāda* school which separated itself from the orthodox sect of the *Theravāda* during Asoke's council (B.C. 240). In this council, the *Abhidharma* literature was recognized as one part of *Tripiṭaka.*[4] The *Theravādins* has preserved seven *Abhidharma* texts in Pāli[5] whereas the *Sarvāstivādins* has left seven *Abhidharma* texts in Chinese translations.[6] Kashmir was the principal center of the *Sarvāstivādins* who respected the *Abhidharma* text of the *Jñānaprasthānaśāstra* as their basic text of study.[7] Six supplementary books known as the six *pādas* (leg) were composed on the subject matters of the *Jñānaprasthāna.* Great commentaries on the *Jñānaprasthāna* - the *Vibhāṣāśāstra,*[8] and the *Mahāvibhāṣāśāstra* (*Nanjio* 1263) - were composed in which various opinion of the time were recorded and analysed. Later on many compendiums of the *Abhidharma* were composed.[9] The *Vibhāṣā* mentions two groups of the *Sarvāstivādin* the "*Kāshmiraśāstrins*" and the "*Gāndhāraśāstrins*" (the *Sarvāstivāda* group that flourished in Gandhara and did not accept the *Jñānaprasthāna* as its basic text). The two groups later merged with each other, as after the composition of the *Mahāvibhāṣāśāstra* only the Kashmir-*Vaibhāṣikas* or the *Vaibhāṣikas* were recognized as the followers of the *Sarvāstivāda.*[10] The fundamental principle of the *Sarvāstivāda* school is *sarvam asti, i-ch'ieh-yu pu*[11] (all exists). It refers to the conviction that the *dharmas* of the three times, past, future, and present exist. Their existence in all times is derived from the continuance of their essence in the time past, present and future.[12]

The missionary zeal of the Kashmiri *Sarvāstivādins* was noticed from the first century A.D. when they made their way to Central Asia and gradually established great centres of the *Sarvāstivada* there in Badakshan, Kashgar and Kucha. These centres formed the Northern Route that came to be the passage for the Buddhist pilgrims from India and Central Asia to proceed to China. Saṅghabhūti[13] is reported to be the first *Sarvāstivāda* monk to arrive in China through this route in A.D. 381. Saṅghadeva, a native of Kubha (Kabul) and a renowned *Ābhidhārmika* teacher in Kashmir, following the same route arrived at Ch'ang-an in north China in A.d. 383. He stayed in different place in China for fifteen years till his death.

II

Ch'ang-an was the capital of north China under the Tibetan ruler Fu Chien. For north China it was a period of political unrest following the fall of Lo-yang to the non-Chinese invaders in A.D. 316. The Confucian scholars and officials fled to south Ching where they set up a new Chinese empire. The new regime of the north needed the assistance of a literate class loyal to them. They found the Buddhists and the Taoists[14] suitable for this purpose. For the Buddhists, they extended special favour to the monks by encouraging translation of the Buddhist texts in Chinese, by building monasteries and by seeking the advice of the monks even in political affairs.[15] In turn, the Buddhist community was eager for royal support in order to consolidate the position of Buddhism in north China in terms of its monastic establishments and missionary activities including the preaching, teaching and the translation of the Buddhist texts. In Chang-an a translation bureau was sponsored by Fu Chien's court under the leadership of the great Chinese Buddhist monk Tao-an.[16] The foreigner monks who came in large number in Chang-an during A.D. 380-385, were invited by Tao-an and Fu Chien's secretary Chao-Cheng, to participate in the translations of the Buddhist texts in Chinese along with the native Chinese monks.[17] After his arrival in Ch'ang-an, Saṅghadeva joined this group of translators.

In Ch'ang-an centre, detailed arrangements were made for the translations of the *Sarvāstivāda* canon. The translations were done jointly by the *Sarvāstivāda* monks namely Saṅghadeva, Saṅghabhūti, and Dharmanandī,[18] in collaboration with the Chinese monk scholars led by Chu Fo-nien.[19] The foreigner monks had little knowledge or no knowledge of Chinese for translation work in China. They recited the Sanskrit texts from memory or presented the manuscripts of the texts which were translated by some scholars well versed both in Chinese and Sanskrit.[20] During A.D. 383-385 Saṅghadeva translated two or three *Sarvāstivāda* texts among which the *Abhidharmajñānapra sthānaśāstra*, the Chinese version of the principal text of the *Sarvāstivāda abhidharma* still exits. *Saṅghadeva* had little knowledge of Chinese and he was helped by Chu Fo-nien in the translation of the *Jñānaprasthāna*. It is also reported that Saṅghadeva forgot the seventh section of the book during his recital of it and the section was omitted. Later it was added by another monk, T'an mo-pi, who met Saṅghadeva and recited the section from memory. Thus the translation of the text was complete.[21]

For China, this was her first acquintance with the scholastic *Abhidharma* doctrines. A couple of elementary *Abhidharma* texts were already translated[22] and they were popular too. But in most cases those texts were not more than just lists of the *Abhidharma* terms. The translation of the *Jñānaprasthāna* by Saṅghadeva opened up the fascinating field of the analysis of the numerical groups and categories of concepts that presented a vast panaroma of the Buddhist world-view. The Chinese had no parallel secular or philosophical literature compared to the *Sarvāstivādā bhidharma*.[23] The impact of the *Abhidharma* along with the *Āgamas* and the *Vinaya* of the *Sarvāstivādins* on the Chinese mind was overwhelming. Earlier devoted to the *Mahāyāna* text of the *Prajñāpāramitā*, Tao-an and his outstanding disciple Hui-yuan developed a strong feeling towards *Sarvāstivāda*.[24] However, with the death of Tao-an and the fall of Fu Chien, the translation activity in Ch'ang-an was decreased.

III

In A.D. 385, A friend and disciple of Tao-an, Fa-ho invited Saṅghadeva to Lo-yang, another important Buddhist centre to check and verify the Chinese translation of the *Ekottarāgama* (*Nanjio*, 543) by Dharmanandī, with the original version of the *Sarvāstivādins.* Saṅghadeva accepted the invitation and went to Lo-yang. He spent four or five years there explaining the *Sarvāstāivada* scriptures and learning Chinese language.[25] As he realized that Buddhism was flourishing more in southern China, he left for south in A.D. 391.

Huiyüan heard of Saṅghadeva's presence, in Hsun-yang in south China and invited him cordially to live in Lu-shan, a famous Buddhist centre in south, where Hui-yuan himself lived and worked. Saṅghadeva accepted the invitation and lived in Lu-shan from A.D. 391 to A.D. 397. He had his own monastery on the southern side of the mountain Lu. Saṅghadeva's lecture on the *Abhidharma* influenced the monks living on Mt. Lu. Hui Yüan requested him to translate the *Abhidharmahṛdaya* (*Nanjio*, 1288) along with the *San fa-tu-lun* (*Nanjio*, 1271).[26] With Hui-yüan's help Saṅghadeva completed the translations. Hui-yüan also wrote prefaces to the texts, in which, he explained the basic purport of the texts.[27]

In A.D. 397 Saṅghadeva proceeded to Chien-kang and his profound learning impressed the official circle there. Wang hsuen, a high official and devout Buddhist built a monastary for him. Saṅghadeva lectured on the *Āgamas* and the *Abhidharma* texts in the monastery and a large gathering of his disciples and high official listened to him. With the assistance of other Kashmiri *Sarvāstivādins* and the Chinese monks, he translated the *Madhyamāgama* (*Nanjio*, 542) and the *Ekottarāgama* (now lost). The *Mahāvibhāṣā* was also translated by him but it is not available now. The end of this great *Sarvāstivādin* scholar came probably in A.D. 398 in south China.

Saṅghadeva successfully completed his mission of introducing *Sarvāstivāda abhidharma* in China. After him the *Abhidharma* learning continued to flourish in China. The *Abhidharmahṛdaya* translated by him had a commentary *Saṃyuktābhidharmahṛdaya* by Dharmatrāta,[28] which was translated into Chinese in A.D. 434 by Saṅghavermā.[29] On the basis of this translation, *Tsā-a-p'i-tan-hsin-lun* (*Nanjio* 1237) the first *Abhidharma* school known as the *A-p'i-t'an-mo-tsung* was established. The school developed in the line of the Gāndhara *Abhidharma* as Dharmatrāta was a follower of the Gāndhara branch of the *Sarvāstivāda*. Following the *Samyuktābhidharmahṛdaya* Vasubandhu wrote the *Abhidharmakośa* which was translated in Chinese by Paramārtha[30] and Hsüan-Tsang.[31] On the basis of Hsüan-Tsang's translation the *Chu-she* school was established by Hsüan-Tsang and his disciple Kuei-ch'i.[32] The *A-p'i-ta-mo* school was merged with the *Chu-she*. Finally the *Chu-she* school was officially registered as a part of the *Dharmalakṣaṇa* or the *Fa-hsiang* school in A.D. 793.[33] *Hsüan-Tsang* translated almost all the principal texts of the *Sarvāstivada abhidharma*. These translations are the only sources for the study of those texts which are not available in their original or Tibetan translations. Thus from the viewpoint of the history of Buddhist philosophy and literature in general Saṅghadeva occupies a prominent place as the pioneer teacher and translator of the *Sarvāstivāda* tradition in China.

Reference :

1. Biography in *Kao-seng-chuan* I, *Taisho* 50, 328c-329a. For other details on Saṅghadeva, see Nanjio, App. ii, 39, P. Bagchi, *Le Cannon Bouddhique on Chine* (Paris, 1927), pp. 161-62, 335; P.K. Mukerjee, *Indian literature in China* (Calcutta, no date of publication), pp. 54-56; B.N. Puri, *Buddhism in Central Asia* (Delhi, 1987), pp. 123-24; Chou Hsiang Kuang, *A History of Chinese*

Buddhism (Allahabad, 1955), p. 43; E. Zürcher, *The Buddhist conquest of China* (Leiden, 1972), pp. 202, 230.

2. Technically *abhidharma* is defined as "higher religion" or "excellent religion" See *Aṭṭhasālini*, I. 2.

3. A.K. Warder, *Indian Buddhism* (Delhi, 1980), pp. 218-224.

4. A.C. Banerjee, *Sarvastivad Literature* (Calcutta, 1979), p. 53.

5. The texts are; *Dhammasaṅgaṇi, Vibhaṅga, Kathāvatthu, Puggalapaññatti, Dhātukathā, Yamaka and Paṭṭhāna.* For details, see B.C. Law, *A History of Pali literature* (Delhi, 1983), pp. 304-335.

6. For details, see A.C. Banerjee, *op. cit.*, pp. 54-69; J. Takakusu, "On the Abhidharma Literature of the Sarvāstivadins, in *Journal of Pali Text Society*" (1905), pp. 86-118.

7. The geographical extension of the *Sarvāstivāda* school is discussed in J. Takakusu, *I-Tsing's record of the Buddhist religion as practised in India and the Malaya Archipelago* (N. Delhi, 1982), pp. xxii-xxiv.

8. The text is available in two Chinese Versions (see *Nanjio* 1299, 1264).

9. The most important among those texts is the *Abhidharmakośa.* For other texts, see Takakusu, *On the Abhidharma literature*, pp. 139-145.

10. *Ibid.*, p. 119.

11. Soothill, *A Dictionary of Chinese Buddhism*, (Delhi, 1977), p. 3a.

12. Cf. *Abhidharmadīpa* (Patna, 1977), *Śloka* 303.

13. For his life see *Nanjio*, App. II. 54.

14. Taoism is a school of Chinese thought represented by Lao Tzu and Chuang Tzu. "Tao" or "the way" is the underlying principle of the universe. Union with the Tao through identification is the goal of life for the Taoists. However, Taoism that developed as religion aims at "material immortality" mainly through respiratory practices and restricted food habits. For the development of Taoism in the fourth and fifth century China, see *The Cambridge History of China*, D. Twitchett and M. Loewe (ed.) (Combridge, 1986), pp. 828-837, 860-868.

15. Monk Tao-an persuaded Fu Chien not to go for a war against south China. For details, see Zürcher, *op. cit.*, p. 201.

16. Biography in *Kao-seng-chuan* 5, *Taisho* 50, 351c-354a.

17. Kenneth Chen, *Buddhism in China*, (Princeton, 1964), pp. 101-102.

18. Biography in *Kao-seng-chuan* I, *Taisho* 50, 328a-b.

19. Biography in *Ibid*, I, 329

20. For early translation technique of the Buddhist texts in China, see Kenneth Chen, *op. cit.*, pp. 366-67.

21. J. Takakusu, "On the Abhidharma literature of the Sarvastivadins" in *Journal of Pali Text Society*, (1905), pp. 94-95.

22. The *Abhidharmapañcakadharmacaryāsūtra* (*Nanjio*, 1346) translated by An Shi-kao in A.D. 148-170, and the *Abhidharmāmrtaśāstra* (*Nanjio*, 1278), translator unknown, translated in A.D. 220-265.

23. Zürcher, *op. cit.*, p. 204.

24. Tao-an wrote a preface on Saṅghabhūti's translation of the *Abhidharmavibhāsāśāstra* and Hui-Yüan wrote a preface on Saṅghadeva's translation of the *Abhidharmahṛdaya.*

25. P. K. Mukerjee, *op. cit.*, p. 54.

26. Translated by Saṅghadeva in collaboration with Hui Yüan in A.D. 391.

27. Zürcher, *op. cit.,* p. 408, note 74.

28. For details see *Nanjio*, App. I. 31.

29. For details see *Ibid*, App. II. 80.

30. For Paramārtha's translation in A.D. 563-567, see *Taisho* 29, No. 1559.

31. For Hsüan-Tsang's translation in A.D. 651-654, see *ibid*, No. 1558.

32. For details on the *Chu-she* school see J. Takakusu, *The Essentials of Buddhist Philosophy* (Delhi, 1975), pp. 55-73.

33. Kenneth Chen, *op.cit.*, p. 303.

SELECT BIBLIOGRAPHY

Original Sources

SANSKRIT AND PĀLI

Abhidharmadīpa with *Vibhāṣaprabhāvṛtti*, (ed) P.S. Jaini, Patna, 1977.

Abhidharmakośa and *Bhāṣya* of Acharya Vasubandhu, Part I and II (ed) Swami Dwarikadas Sastri, Varanasi, 1981.

Abhidharmāmṛta of Ghoṣaka, (Tr) from Chinese into Sanskrit, by Shanti Bhiksu Sastri, Santiniketan, 1958.

Abhidharmasamuccaya by Asaṅga, Pradhan, Santiniketan, 1950.

Aṅguttaranikāya, (ed.) Morris and Hardy in 5 Vols., PTS, 1885-1900.

Dhātukathā and *Puggalapaññatti*, (ed.) Bhikkhu J. Kasyap, Bihar, 1960.

Dīghanikāya, (ed.) T.W. Rhys Davids and J.E. Carpenter in 3 Vols., PTS, 1890-1911.

Jñānaprasthānaśāstra, (Tr.) from Chinese into Sanskrit by Shanti Bhiksu Sastri, Santiniketan, 1955.

Mahāvyutpatti, Bibliotheca Buddhica XIII, 1911.

Mahayānasūtrālamkāra by Asaṅga, (ed) Swami Dwarikadas Sastri, Bauddha Bharati, Varanasi, 1985.

Majjhimanikāya, (ed.) Trenchner and Chalmers in 3 Vols, PTS 1889-99, reprinted 1948-51.

Samyuttanikāya, (ed.) Feer in 5 Vols., PTS 1884-98, reprinted 1960.

Vibhaṅga, (ed.) Bhikkhu J. Kashyap, Bihar, 1960.

CHINESE

A-p'i-ta-mo-chieh-shen-tsu-lun, (tr.) Hsüan-tsang, A.D. 663, T. 1540.

A-p'i-ta-mo-chü-she-lun-pen-sung, (tr) Hsüan-tsang, A.D. 651, T-1560.

A-p 'i-ta-mo-fa-yün-tsu-lun, (tr.) Hsüan-tsang, A.D. 659, T. 1536.

A- p'i - t a-mo-p'in lei-tsulun, (tr.) Hsüan-tsang, A.D. 649, T. 1542.

Taisho shinshu daizokyo, (ed) Takakusu Junjiro, 55 Vols (Tokyo, 1914-22).

Ch'eng-wei-shih-lun by Hsüan-tsang, A.D. 659, T. 1586.

Secondary Sources

Aung, S.Z. and Rhys Davids, C.A.F., tr. *Points of Controversy* (*Kathāvatthu*), PTS, 1915.

Banerjee, A.C. : *Sarvāstivāda Literature*, Calcutta, 1957.

The Book of Analysis (*Vibhaṅga*), The Second Book of the *Abhidhamma Piṭaka* (Translated from the Pāli of the Burmese Chaṭṭhasaṅgīti Edition) Published for the Pali Text Society, London by Luzac and Co., London, 1969.

Beal, Samuel, *Si-yu-ki-Buddhist Records of the Western World*, Reprint, Delhi, 1981.

Carpenter, J.E. and Rhys David, T.W. (eds) : *Dīgha Nikāya*, 3 Vols., PTS, 1889-1910.

Chalmers, R. Trenckner, V. and Rhys Davids, C.A.F. (eds) :

Majjhima Nikāya, 4 Vols., PTS, 1889-1925.

Chandhury, Sukomal, *Analytical Study of the Abhidharmakośa*, Calcutta, 2nd ed., 1983.

Chau, Thich Minh, *The Chinese Madhyama Āgama and the Pāli Majjhima Nikāya*, Delhi, 1991.

Davids Rhys, *The Birth of Indian Psychology and its Development in Buddhism*, First Indian Edition, 1978. - *A Buddhist Manual of Psychological Ethics*, First Indian Edition, Delhi, 1975.

Dutt, N. *The Spread of Buddhism and the Buddhist Schools*, First Indian Edition 1980.

Dietz Siglinde, "Investigation for the similarity of the school of thoughts of the Gilgit - fragments preserved in Ujjain (in German) in *Zür Schulzugehörigkeit von Werken der Hīnayāna Literature*, Gottingen, 1985. —*Fragments des Dharmaskandha, Gottingen*, 1984

Edgerton, *Buddhist Hybrid Sanskrit Dictionary*, Yale University Press, 1953.

Guenther, Herbert V. : *Philosophy and Psychology in the Abhidharma*, Motilal Banarasidass, Delhi 1957.

Halder, Aruna : *Some Psychological Aspects of Early Buddhist Philosophy* Based on *Abhidharmakośa* of Vasubandhu, The Asiatic Society, Calcutta, 1981.

Hardy, E. and Morris, R. (ed) : *Aṅguttara Nikāya*, 6 Vols.,

Feer, L. and Rhys Davids, C.A.F. (ed) : *Aṅguttara Nikāya*, 6 Vols., PTS, 1885-1910.

Ganguly Swati, *Treatise in Groups of Elements*, Delhi, 1994.

Hare, E.M. and Woodward, P.L. (tr.), *The Book of Gradual Sayings* (*Aṅguttara Nikāya*), 5 Vols., PTS, 1932-1936.

Jayatilleke, K.N., *Early Buddhist Theory of Knowledge, London,* 1963, MLBD (Reprint), 1981.

Hinuber, O.V, *Die Erforschung des Gilgit Handschriften* (The Research of the Gilgit Manuscripts), *Nachrichten der Akademie der Wissenschaften* in Gottingern, 1979, No. 12.

Karunaratna Upali, "Dharmaskandha" in *Encyclopedia of Buddhism,* Vol. IV, Fascicle 4, Ed. A.W.P. Guruge and W.G. Weeraratne, 1989, p. 560.

Law, Bimala Charan : *A history of Pāli Literature,* Indological Book House, Delhi, 1983.

Ling, Trevor, *A Dictionary of Buddhism* (Indian and Southeast Asian), K.P. Bagchi and Co., Calcutta, 1978.

Masuda, J. "Origins and doctrines of Early Buddhist schools" in *Asia Major,* 2 : 1-78.

Mathews, R.H. : *Chinese - English Dictionary,* Cambridge, 1975.

Monier-Williams, Sir Monier : *A Sanskrit - English Dictionary,* Motilal Banarasidass, Delhi, 1986.

Nanjio, Bunyiu, *A Catalogue of the Chinese Translation of the Buddhist Tripiṭaka,* New Delhi edition, 1980.

Narada U, *Discourse on Elements,* PTS, 1977.

Nariman, J.K. *Literary History of Sanskrit Buddhism,* Reprint, Delhi, 1972.

Nyanatiloka : *Buddhist Dictionary : Manual of Buddhist Terms and Doctrines,* Frewin and Co., Colombo, 1972.

Pandeya, R. (ed.) *Buddhist Studies in India,* Delhi, 1975.

Poussin, Louis de La Vallée : *Abhidharma-Kośabhāṣyam* (English translation by Leo M. Pruden) Vols. I, II, III and IV, Asian Humanities Press, Berkeley, California, 1989-90.

Sasaki, Genjun H. *Linguistic Approach to Buddhist Thought*, 2nd edition, Delhi, 1992.

Sinha, Braj M. : *Time and Temporality in Sāmkhya-Yoga and Abhidharma Buddhism*, Munshiram Manoharlal Publishers, New Delhi, 1983.

Stcherbatsky, Th. : *The Central Conception of Buddhism and the Meaning of the Word of "Dharma"*, Motilal Banarasidass, Delhi, 1983.

Takakusu, J., "On the Abhidharma Literature of the *Sarvāstivādins*" in the *Journal of Pali Text Society*, 1905.

Tatia, N. "Sarvāstivād" in the *Nava Nalanda Mahavihara Research Publication*, Vol. II, p. 77.

Thera, Nyanaponika : *Abhidhamma Studies - Researches in Buddhist Psychology*, Buddhist Publication Soceity, Kandy, Sri Lanka, 1985.

Upadhyaya, Baladev, *Bauddha - Darśana - Mīmāmsā* (in Hindi), Varanasi, 1978.

Warder, A.K. : *Indian Buddhism*, Motilal Banarasidass, Delhi, 1980.

Dutt, Nalinaksha : *Mayāyāna Buddhism*, Motilal Banarsidass, Delhi, 1978.

Watanabe, Fumimaro : *Philosophy and its Development in the Nikāyas and Abhidhamma*, Motilal Banarasidass, Delhi, 1983.

Watanbe, K. And Takakusu, J. (eds) : *Taishō*, 55 Vols., Tokyo, 1924-1929.

Watters, T., *On Yuan-Chuwang's travel in India*, Second Indian Edition, Delhi, 1973.

Winternitz, M. *History of Indian Literature*, Reprint, Delhi, 1983.

INDEX